Paper Piecing Picnic

Fun-Filled Projects for Every Quilter

From the
Editors and Contributors of
Quilter's Newsletter Magazine
and *Quiltmaker*

C&T PUBLISHING

© 2001 Primedia Special Interest Publications

Editor: Diane Kennedy-Jackson, Lynn Koolish, Jan Grigsby
Copy Editor: Carol Barrett
Book Designer: Michael Rohani
Design Director: Diane Pedersen
Cover Design & Production: Christina D. Jarumay
Production Assistant: Kirstie L. McCormick
Photography: Mellisa Karlin Mahoney
Cover Image: *Colorful Kites* by Joyce A. Robinson

Attention Teachers:
C&T Publishing, Inc. encourages you to use this book as a text for teaching. Contact us at
800-284-1114 or www.ctpub.com for more information about the C&T Teachers Program.

Library of Congress Cataloging-in-Publication Data

Paper Piecing Picnic : Fun-Filled Projects for Every Quilter / from the editors and
contributors of *Quilter's Newsletter Magazine* and *Quiltmaker* Magazine ; editor,
Diane Kennedy-Jackson.
      p. cm.
   ISBN 1-57120-144-0
   1. Quilting–Patterns. 2. Patchwork–Patterns. I. Kennedy-Jackson, Diane
II. *Quilter's Newsletter Magazine.* III. *Quiltmaker.*
   TT835 .P3513 2002
   746.46'041–dc21

                                                      2001006147

Published by C&T Publishing, Inc.
P.O. Box 1456
Lafayette, California 94549

Printed in Singapore
10 9 8 7 6 5 4 3 2 1

Introduction

The editors of C & T Publishing are pleased to bring *Paper Piecing Picnic* to quilters everywhere.

Whether you are an experienced quiltmaker or you're just getting started, you're certain to find the ideal projects to get your creativity flowing in this collection of sixteen paper-piecing designs.

Including selected favorites from *Quiltmaker Magazine* and *Quilter's Newletter Magazine*, this collection contains designs from beginning to challenging, from whimsical to breathtaking. Projects featuring everything from the classic Pickle Dish block design to decorative appliqué are included. Also included are designs that are ideal for youngsters. What better way to get a little one interested in quilting than to present him or her with a cozy warmer or colorful wall art? Know a member of the younger set who loves dinosaurs? *Rick Rackosaurus* is sure to bring delight!

Whether you fancy vibrant color or intricate design, you're certain to find a variety of projects you'll be anxious to begin, whether you plan to use them in your own home or present them to loved ones. So sit back, relax, peruse the pages of *Paper Piecing Picnic,* and reach for your fabric stash. Happy quiltmaking!

Contents

Paper-Foundation Piecing 101	6
Projects:	8
Rick Rackosaurus	8
Puzzled	13
Colorful Kites	17
Party Whirl	22
Garden Patch	26
Secret Garden	32
Wee Houses	39
Fireworks	43
Pineapple Slices	47
Sunflowers	52
Pink Dogwood	57
Trip to New York	63
Dandelion	67
Indian Wedding Ring	72
Apache Trail	76
Thanksgiving Wedding Ring	80
Quilting Basics	87
Index	91

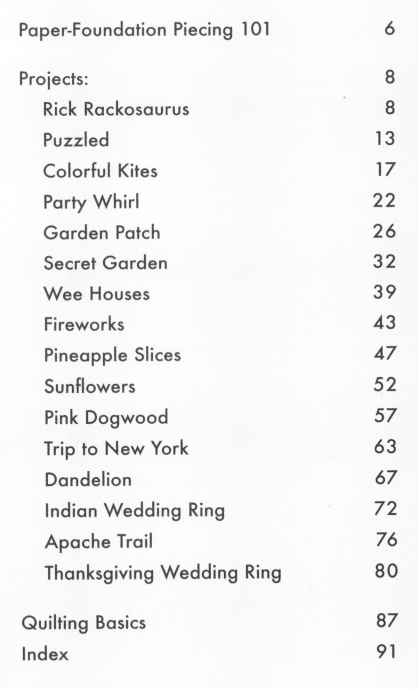

Paper-Foundation Piecing 101

by Barbara Fiedler

Foundation-piecing is an accurate technique for sewing blocks that are difficult to piece. A little practice and knowing a few "do's and don'ts" will make you successful with this popular technique.

To help you understand this piecing method, study this foundation-pieced block and the illustrations of common foundation-piecing mistakes. For instruction, the correct stitching is shown in black and incorrect sewing is marked in red. It doesn't take long to master this technique; you'll be passing PFP 101 in one easy lesson.

1. **Trace or photocopy the complete foundation pattern, including all the numbers and lines.** Without the block seam lines or cutting lines, you will not know where to sew or where to trim the block to its correct size.

2. **Cut out the paper foundation beyond the outer line.** The extra dimension is a good visual measure of size for those patches that lie along the block perimeter. If your patches extend beyond the foundation, you know they will be large enough.

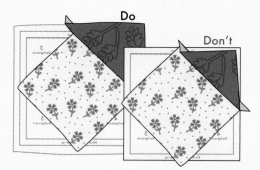

3. **Always set your stitch length to a short setting, 18–20 stitches to the inch.** Longer stitches won't perforate the paper close enough so it will be

harder to tear away the foundation and easier for the stitches to pull loose.

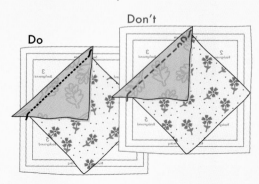

4. **Check patch placement before you sew it to the foundation.** If not, you could sew a patch with a seam allowance that is too narrow or miss sewing the patch to the foundation.

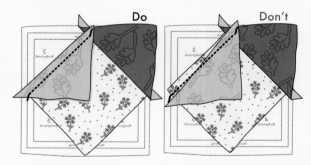

5. **Stitch on the printed side of the foundation to easily follow the sewing line and sew exactly on the printed seam line.** Sewing off the line will change the pattern or design.

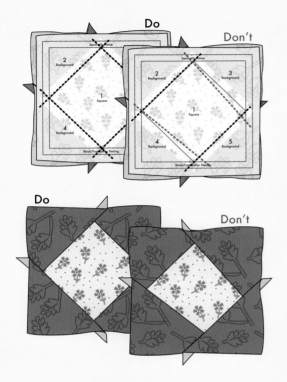

6. **For every seam line, begin stitching ¼" before the seam line and continue ¼" beyond.** If the stitching does not cross over the previous seam line, as consecutive patches are added a gap will exist in the patchwork. Backstitching does not take the place of cross seaming.

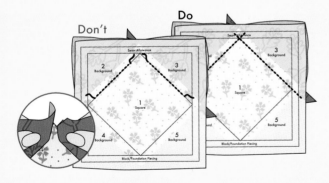

7. **After each patch addition, trim the seam allowances to ¼".** Narrower seam allowances can pull away from the stitching and leave a hole in the block.

8. **After a patch is added, open the patch from the fabric side and press the seam flat.** Otherwise, you will have a tuck in the fabric and patches will not be the correct size.

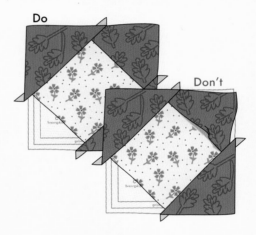

9. **Trim the foundation precisely on the outside line after it is pieced.** Careless cutting will give an inaccurate size block.

10. **Leave the outer foundation lines unsewn.** If you stitch the foundation perimeter, removing the paper will be difficult.

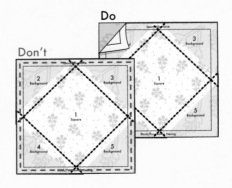

PLEASE NOTE: Photocoping may cause distortion. Compare pattern copies to original for accuracy.

Rick Rackosaurus

By Joyce Robinson

Dinosaurs in a fireworks display of riotous fabrics were the goal for *Rick Rackosaurus!* Selecting the border fabric first made it easy to choose dinosaur fabric for this eye-popping, bold, and brilliantly colored children's quilt.

Designed by *Quilter's Newsletter Magazine* staff artist Joyce Robinson. Sewn by Peg Spradlin.

MATERIALS AND CUTTING

Block Size:		4½"
Quilt Size:		27" x 27"

Requirements are based on 42" fabric width.

Borders include 2" extra length plus seam allowances.

Read all instructions before cutting.

Materials	Yards	Cutting
Pink Print	1/8	
setting squares		32 #2 patch
Dark Multiprint	1/8	
setting squares		16 #1 patch
Red Print	1/4	
inner borders		4 at 1¼" x 23½"
Teal Print	1/2	
binding		3 strips 2¼" x 42"
sashes		24 sashes
Bright Multiprint*	7/8	
outer borders		4 at 3½" x 29½"
For each block-foundation pattern:		
Solid Scraps		
Y block:		
dinosaur's "snout"		2" x 4"
background patches		9" x 9"
Z block:		
dinosaur's legs		2" x 6"
background patches		3" x 16"
Print Scraps		
Y block:		
dinosaur's body		7" x 8"
Z block:		
dinosaur's body		4" x 6"
Backing	7/8	
backing		1 panel 29" x 29"
sleeve		9" x 27"
Batting		4" longer and wider than quilt top

Supplies: Black embroidery floss and 8" of jumbo rickrack per block

* Yardage given is for lengthwise strips. To cut the borders from selvage to selvage, only ½ yard of fabric will be needed.

GETTING STARTED

Wash and press fabrics. Cut the patches and other pieces as listed in the materials and cutting box. Refer to page 87 for Quilting Basics.

MAKING THE BLOCKS

1. Trace or photocopy five Y blocks, four Z blocks, and sixteen volcano setting squares.

2. For each Y block, foundation-piece patches 1–16 in numerical order. For each Z block, foundation-piece patches 1–14 in numerical order.

3. Before adding the remaining pieces, sew a basting stitch along the rickrack placement line of each block, creating a placement line on the fabric.

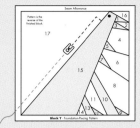 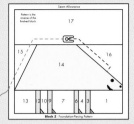

4. Fold the end of the rickrack nearest the head as shown, aligning the points along the basting stitches. Sew the rickrack in place ⅛" from the basting stitches.

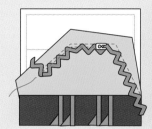 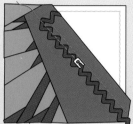

5. Sew remaining patches in place. Press the rickrack away from the dinosaurs' bodies.

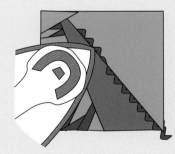

6. Make five Y blocks and four Z blocks.
7. Sew the volcano setting squares, sewing fabric units in numerical order.
8. Make sixteen volcano setting squares.

ASSEMBLING THE QUILT TOP

1. Make four rows of sash, plus two of Row 1, and one of Row 2, referring to row assembly.

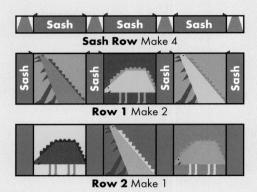

Sash Row Make 4

Row 1 Make 2

Row 2 Make 1

Row Assembly

2. Remove the paper.
3. Press the seam allowances toward the sashes.
4. Embroider facial features as shown on patterns, using two strands of floss. Make French knots for eyes, wrapping the needle four times. Make French knots for noses, wrapping the needle twice. Use Outline stitch to make the mouths (refer to page 11).
5. Join the rows, alternating row types.
6. Press the seam allowances in one direction.
7. Sew inner and outer borders together to make four border units. Sew border units to the sides of the quilt. Sew border units to the top and bottom, mitering the corners. Press the seam allowances toward the borders.

QUILTING AND FINISHING

1. Mark the fossil-feet quilting motifs as shown, referring to quilting placement.

Quilting Placement

2. Layer the quilt backing, batting, and top.

3. Baste.

4. Quilt the sashes, setting squares, and borders in-the-ditch. Quilt the fossil-feet motifs.

5. Trim quilt backing and batting even with the quilt top.

6. Join 2¼"-wide strips end to end to make the binding.

7. Bind the quilt.

8. Sew a sleeve to the backing for display purposes.

9. Refer to Label-O-Saurus instructions to make a label.

SNAKE IN THE GRASS

Snakes and lizards make many people squeamish, but dinosaurs, those extinct members of the reptile family, seem to be loved by all.

Whether created with the bold and playful colors of the quilt on page 8, or in the more muted colors shown here, these dinosaurs are sure to escape extinction!

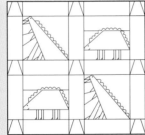

LABEL-O-SAURUS

Let this wide-mouthed dinosaur help bring to extinction the notation "quiltmaker unknown."

Pin fabric for #1 patch in place and sew a basting stitch along the rickrack placement lines. Sew pieces of medium rickrack in place ⅛" from the basting stitches. Join fabrics for #2 and #3 patches together, then sew them to the foundation. Sew the remaining patches in numerical order. Remove the paper. Embroider the details. Putting words in the dino's mouth, mark your name and

date with a fabric-marking pen. Sew the label to the backing.

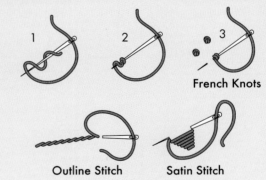

French Knots

Outline Stitch   Satin Stitch

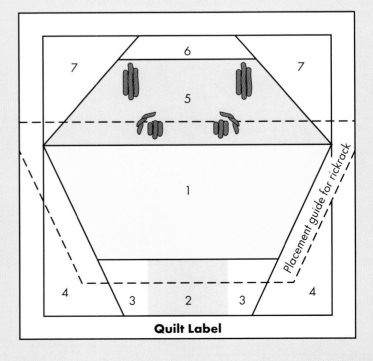

Quilt Label

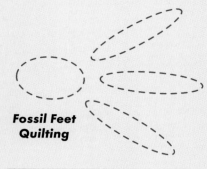

Fossil Feet Quilting

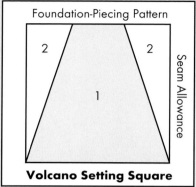

Foundation-Piecing Pattern

Seam Allowance

2   2

1

Volcano Setting Square

Make 16

Rotary Cutting

Measurements include ¼" seam allowance. Align arrow with lengthwise or crosswise grain of fabric.

2"

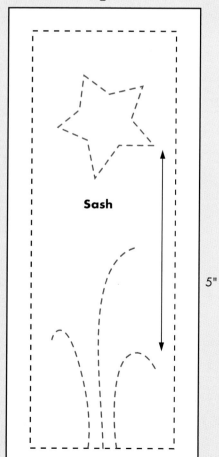

Sash

5"

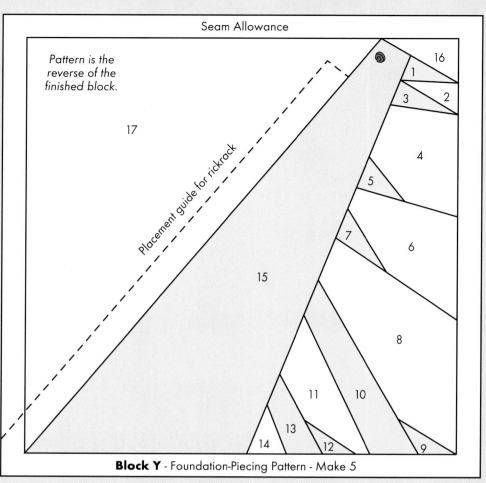

Seam Allowance

Pattern is the reverse of the finished block.

17

16

1

3   2

4

5

7   6

15

8

11   10

13

14   12   9

Placement guide for rickrack

Block Y - Foundation-Piecing Pattern - Make 5

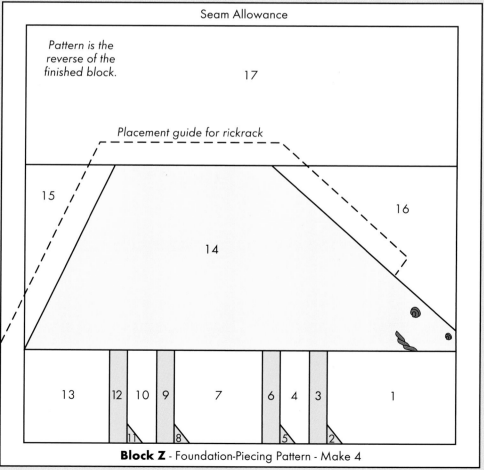

Seam Allowance

Pattern is the reverse of the finished block.

17

Placement guide for rickrack

15   16

14

13   12 10 9   7   6 4 3   1

11   8   5   2

Block Z - Foundation-Piecing Pattern - Make 4

Puzzled

By Kathy DeWeese

Simple, geometric blocks take on a tessellated, puzzle-piece appearance in Kathy DeWeese's appropriately named quilt, *Puzzled*. The fabric placement, along with triple-ring quilting, gives the blocks the appearance of being much more complicated than they really are.

The designer used a variety of red, white, and blue fabrics for her patriotic-looking quilt. This design would also be well-suited to a variety of additional color schemes, ranging from favorite colors to those that would match the décor of a home.

Designed by Kathy DeWeese. Sewn by Jenny Hubbard.

MATERIALS AND CUTTING

Block Sizes:		13½"	13½"
Quilt Sizes: Sofa Quilt (shown), [Long Twin Comforter]		54" x 67½"	[67½" x 94½"]

Requirements are based on 42" fabric width.

Read all instructions before cutting.

Materials	Yards	Cutting	Materials	Yards	Cutting
Sofa Quilt			**Long Twin Comforter**		
White Print	1¾	40 each #1, 10 patches	**White Print**	2⅞	72 #1 patches; 68 #10 patches
Light Blue Print	2½	40 each #2, 4, 6, 8, 9 patches	**Light Blue Print**	4⅜	68 each #2, 4, 6, 8 patches; 72 #9 patches
Navy Print	3¾		**Navy Print**	5⅞	
binding		7 strips 2¼" x 42"	binding		9 strips 2¼" x 42"
foundation-piecing		40 each #2–9 patches	foundation-piecing		72 each #2, 4, 6, 8 patches; 68 each #3, 5, 7, 9 patches
Red Print	2⅜	40 each #1, 3, 5, 7, 10 patches	**Red Print**	4⅛	68 #1 patches; 72 each #3, 5, 7, 10 patches
Backing	3½	2 panels 37" x 58"	**Backing**	5⅞	2 panels 37" x 99"
Batting		4" longer and wider than quilt top	**Batting**		4" longer and wider than quilt top

Directions are for both the sofa quilt and the long twin comforter. Information that differs for the twin size is given in [ ].

GETTING STARTED

Wash and press fabrics. Cut the patches and other pieces as listed in the materials and cutting box. Refer to page 87 for Quilting Basics.

MAKING THE BLOCKS

1. Trace or photocopy 80 [140] of the foundation-piecing pattern.

2. Foundation-piece four sections, sewing the fabric units in numerical order and referring to the Y block piecing for color placement. Sew sections together, orienting them as shown.

3. Make 10 [18] Y blocks.

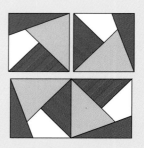

Block Y Piecing
Make 10 [18]

4. Foundation-piece four sections, sewing the fabric units in numerical order and referring to the Z block piecing for color placement. Sew sections together, orienting them as shown.

5. Make 10 [17] Z blocks.

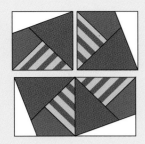

Block Z Piecing
Make 10 [17]

ASSEMBLING THE QUILT TOP

1. Join the Y and Z blocks, referring to row assembly. Make three [four] of row 1 and two [three] of row 2. Press the seam allowances as indicated in row assembly.

Row 1 Make 3 [4]

Row 2 Make 2 [3]

Sofa quilt is shown in darker colors.
Long twin comforter includes the complete diagram.

2. Join the rows, beginning with row 1 and alternating row types.

3. Remove the paper.

QUILTING AND FINISHING

1. Trace the ¼ triple-ring quilting motif from the foundation-piecing pattern, rotating the pattern as needed to complete the design and centering the motif in each block. Refer to quilting

placement. For a traditional marking method, refer to Kitchen Help.

Quilting Placement

2. Layer the quilt backing, batting, and top.

3. Baste.

4. Quilt the seam lines between the blocks in-the-ditch. Quilt the motifs.

5. Trim quilt backing and batting even with the quilt top.

6. Join 2¼"-wide strips end to end to make the binding.

7. Bind the quilt.

KITCHEN HELP

For this old-time technique, find three plates or pan lids of different diameters from your kitchen supplies. Check to see that they will all fit within the block. Center the largest plate within a block and mark the perimeter. Repeat, using the remaining plates. No need to worry if the rings are not equally spaced—odd spacing will only add a traditional flavor. Mark all the blocks using the same plates or, for a different look, vary the size or number of plates.

 TIP

Fabric Tip

- To create the illusion of striped fabric, the stripes are "built-in" to the foundation-piecing pattern. For the stripe patches, fabrics that contrast in value add more spin to the block.

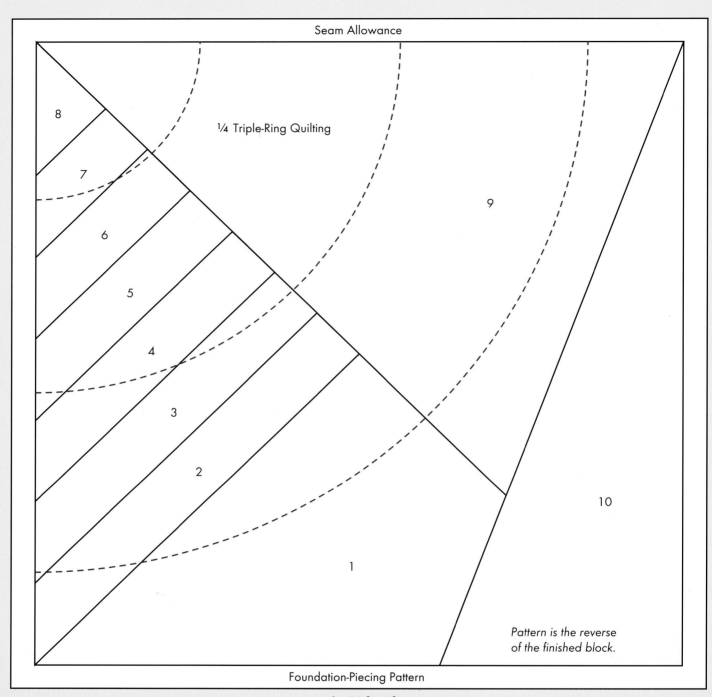

Seam Allowance

8

7

¼ Triple-Ring Quilting

6

9

5

4

3

2

10

1

Pattern is the reverse
of the finished block.

Foundation-Piecing Pattern

Make 80 [140]

Colorful Kites

By Joyce Robinson

What versatile little kites! By reversing some of the foundation patterns and skipping some of the lines when piecing, a variety of kites can be made from just two patterns.

By enlarging the foundation patterns on a photocopier at 150%, the same breezy look can be presented on a quilt large enough for a twin bed.

GETTING STARTED

Wash and press fabrics. Cut the patches and other pieces as listed in the materials and cutting box. Refer to page 87 for Quilting Basics.

Designed by *Quilter's Newsletter Magazine* senior designer Joyce Robinson.
Sewn by Terri Hartline-Belke. Quilted by Penny Wolf.

MATERIALS AND CUTTING

Block Sizes:	6", 6" x 9"	[9", 9" x 13½"]
Quilt Sizes: Crib/Wall Quilt , Twin Comforter (shown)	46" x 57"	[69" x 85½"]

Requirements are based on 42" fabric width.

Borders and sashes include 2" extra length plus seam allowances.

Read all instructions before cutting.

Materials	Yards	Cutting
Crib/Wall Quilt		
White/Gray Print	2⅝	
inner borders (sides)		2 at 2½" x 51½"
inner borders (top/bottom)		2 at 2½" x 44½"
sashes		4 at 2½" x 51½"
A patches		3 at 6½" x 2½"
B patches		3 at 6½" x 8½"
C patch		1 at 6½" x 3½"
D patches		3 at 6½" x 4½"
E patches		4 at 6½" x 5½"
F patches		2 at 6½" x 9½"
G patch		1 at 6½" x 7½"
H patches		2 at 6½" x 3"
I patches		2 at 6½" x 6½"
Bright Scraps		
kites		17 at 9" x 22"
Border Print	1⅝	
outer borders (sides)		2 at 2½" x 55½"
outer borders (top/bottom)		2 at 2½" x 48½"
binding		5 strips 2¼" x 46"
Backing	3	
backing		2 panels 31" x 50"
sleeve for wall quilt		9" x 46"
Batting		4" longer and wider than quilt top

Materials	Yards	Cutting
Twin Comforter		
White/Gray Print	4	
inner borders (sides)		2 at 3½" x 76"
inner borders (top/bottom)		2 at 3½" x 65½"
sashes		4 at 3½" x 76"
A patches		3 at 9½" x 3½"
B patches		3 at 9½" x 12½"
C patch		1 at 9½" x 5"
D patches		3 at 9½" x 6½"
E patches		4 at 9½" x 8"
F patches		2 at 9½" x 14"
G patch		1 at 9½" x 11"
H patches		2 at 9½" x 4¼"
I patches		2 at 9½" x 9½"
Bright Scraps		
kites		17 at 18" x 22"
Border Print	2½	
outer borders (sides)		2 at 3½" x 82"
outer borders (top/bottom)		2 at 3½" x 71½"
binding		5 strips 2¼" x 67"
Backing	5⅜	
backing		2 panels 37" x 90"
sleeve for wall quilt		none for this size
Batting		4" longer and wider than quilt top

Supplies: #5 pearl cotton in variegated purple

Supplies: #5 pearl cotton in variegated purple

Directions are for both the crib/wall quilt and the twin comforter. Information that differs for the twin size is given in [ ].

MAKING THE BLOCKS

1. Trace or photocopy eleven Y blocks, four Z blocks, and four reversed Z blocks. [Enlarge the patterns to 150%.]

2. Foundation-piece the fabric blocks in numerical order. For the most economical use of fabric, piece the blocks that have the largest patches first, in the order shown. For Z blocks, press seam allowances open between sections 1 and 2 after joining the sections.

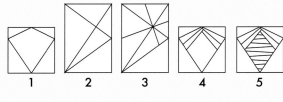

3. Make eleven Y blocks and eight Z blocks.

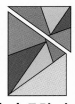

Block Z Piecing
Make 8

Fabric Tips

- For the white/gray print, the dimensions for A–1 patches depend on which size quilt is being made. Before cutting the patches, cut four strips 6½" wide [five strips 9½" wide] from selvage to selvage. From these strips, cut the A–1 patches to the sizes listed in the materials and cutting box.

- Each foundation pattern makes several kite styles. To eliminate confusion while making the blocks, first use a bright-color felt-tip marker to highlight the sewing lines you will use for that block.

ASSEMBLING THE QUILT TOP

1. Join the blocks and patches to make vertical rows, referring to the crib/wall quilt and twin comforter assembly. Make one of each row, pressing the seam allowances toward the plain patches.

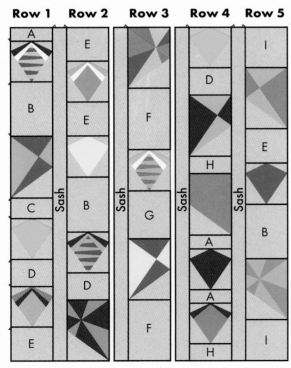

Crib/Wall Quilt and Twin Comforter Assembly

2. Sew a sash to row 3 and press as shown. Trim the sash even with the block row. Measure the length of the sewn sash and trim the remaining three sashes to match. Working from the center outward, join the rows and sashes in the order shown, easing the rows to fit if necessary.

3. Sew the inner borders to the sides of the quilt and trim. Sew the inner borders to the top and bottom and trim. Press the seam allowances toward the borders.

4. Sew the outer borders to the sides of the quilt and trim. Sew the outer borders to the top and bottom and trim. Press the seam allowances toward the borders.

5. Remove the paper.

QUILTING AND FINISHING

1. Freehand mark the quilting lines on the blocks, sashes, and inner border. Following the quilting lines exactly as shown in the quilting placement is not critical. For the wavy diagonal lines, a template can be made from adding-machine paper on a roll. To use this method, cut a 50"-long [75"-long] piece of paper and trim both long sides to make wavy edges. Lay the paper diagonally on the quilt top and pin in place. Trace along the edges. For variation in the lines, turn the paper around or turn it over each time it is repositioned.

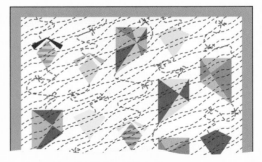

Quilting Placement

2. Layer the quilt backing, batting, and top.

3. Baste.

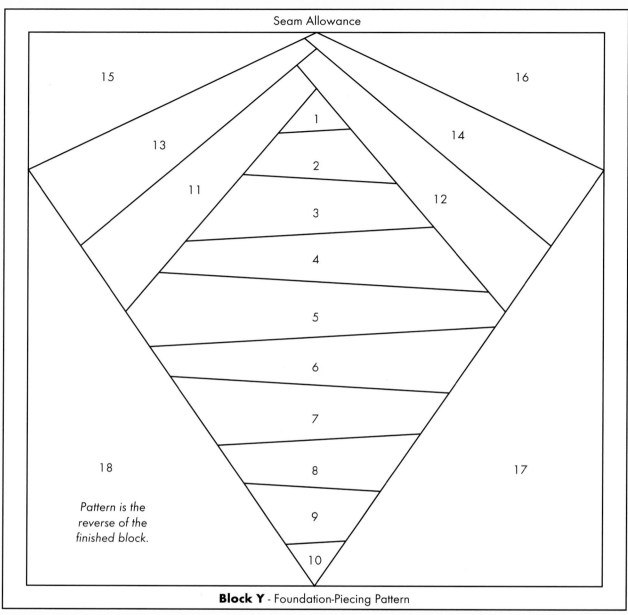

Seam Allowance

15 16

13

1

14

2

11

3

12

4

5

6

7

18

8

17

Pattern is the reverse of the finished block.

9

10

Block Y - Foundation-Piecing Pattern

Make 11

4. Quilt the wavy diagonal lines to suggest a gentle breeze, ending at the outer border seams.

5. Quilt the outer border seams in-the-ditch.

6. Quilt the thread-tails motifs by hand, using pearl cotton and a large stitch (only four to five stitches per inch) to highlight the motifs. (A size 5 quilting between needle has an eye large enough to accommodate the thickness of the pearl cotton.) Refer to the quilting detail.

Quilt the tails, knotting the pearl cotton tightly and carefully burying the thread ends.

7. Trim quilt backing and batting even with the quilt top.

8. Join 2¼"-wide strips end to end to make the binding.

9. Bind the quilt.

10. Sew a sleeve to the backing of the small quilt for display purposes.

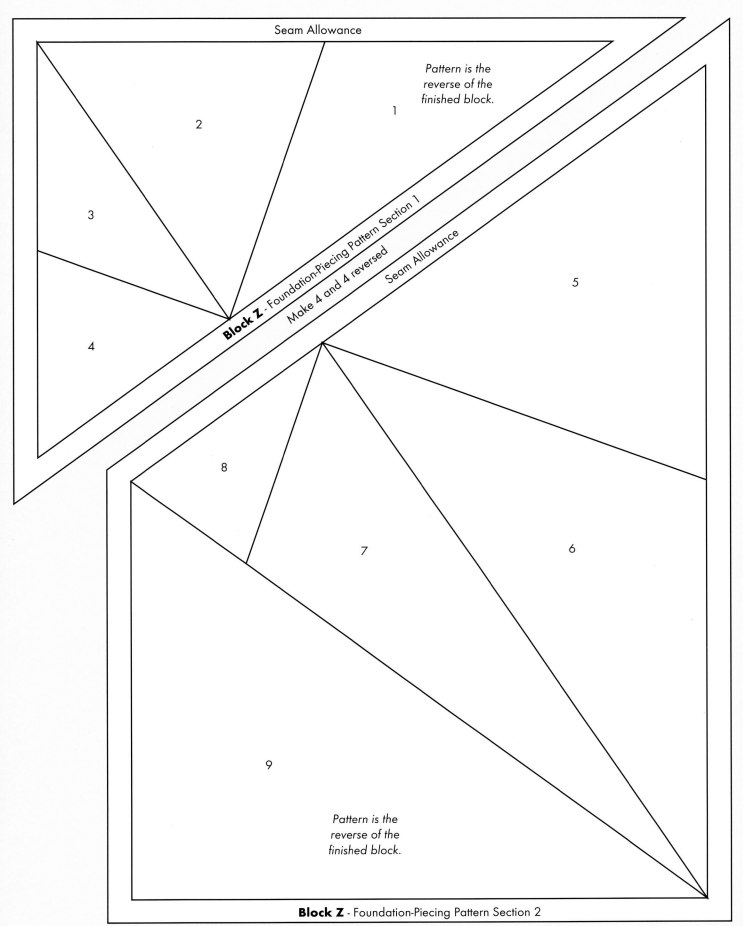

Seam Allowance

Pattern is the
reverse of the
finished block.

1

2

3

4

Block Z - Foundation-Piecing Pattern Section 1

Make 4 and 4 reversed

Seam Allowance

5

8

7

6

9

Pattern is the
reverse of the
finished block.

Block Z - Foundation-Piecing Pattern Section 2

Make 4 and 4 reversed

Party Whirl

BEGINNING ▶

By Linda Schiffer

Linda Schiffer of Columbia, Maryland, enjoys designing foundation-piecing patterns on her computer.

Party Whirl was created as she was experi-menting with color and motion. Linda notes that this quilt reminds her of the dizzying effects of her first dance parties when she was a young girl in middle school.

Designed by Linda Schiffer. Made by Terri Belke.

MATERIALS AND CUTTING

Block Size:		12"
Quilt Size:		63" x 87"

Requirements are based on 42" fabric width.

Borders include 2" extra length plus seam allowances.

Read all instructions before cutting.

Materials	Yards	Cutting
Green Print	1 1/8	96 #6 patches
Light Teal Print	2 5/8	
inner borders (side)		2 at 3" x 74 1/2"
inner borders (top/bottom)		2 at 3" x 55 1/2"
		96 #1 patches
Medium Teal Print	1 1/2	96 #4 patches
Blue Multiprint	3 5/8	
outer borders (sides)		2 at 5 1/4" x 79 1/2"
outer borders (top/bottom)		2 at 5 1/4" x 65 1/2"
		96 #2 patches
Blue Print #1	2 3/4	
binding		4 strips 6" x 85"
		96 #5 patches
Blue Print #2	2 1/8	96 #3 patches
Backing	5 3/8	2 panels 34" x 91"
Batting		4" longer and wider than quilt top

GETTING STARTED

Wash and press fabrics. Cut the patches and other pieces as listed in the materials and cutting box. Refer to page 87 for Quilting Basics.

MAKING THE BLOCKS

1. Trace or photocopy ninety-six units.
2. Foundation-piece the fabric units in numerical order, referring to unit and color key for fabric placement.

Unit
Make 96

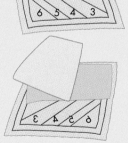

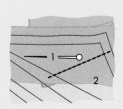

▨ Medium Teal		▢ Light Teal	
▨ Blue #1		▨ Blue Multiprint	
▢ Green		▨ Blue #2	

3. Make ninety-six units.

4. Join four units to make one block, referring to block piecing.

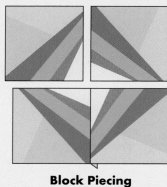

Block Piecing
Make 24

5. Make twenty-four blocks.
6. Remove the paper.

ASSEMBLING THE QUILT TOP

1. Make six rows of four blocks each.
2. Press the seam allowances of every other row in the same direction.
3. Join the rows.
4. Sew the inner borders to the sides of the quilt and trim. Sew the inner borders to the top and bottom and trim. Press the seam allowances toward the borders.

5. Sew the outer borders to the sides of the quilt and trim. Sew the outer borders to the top and bottom and trim. Press the seam allowances toward the borders.

QUILTING AND FINISHING

1. Layer the quilt backing, batting, and top.
2. Baste.
3. Quilt the seam lines between the blocks, the seam lines of patches #1, #2, and #3, and the seam lines between patches #4 and #5 in-the-ditch, referring to quilting placement. Quilt the borders ½" from each seam line and 1¾" from the outer edge.

Quilting Placement

4. Trim quilt backing and batting even with the quilt top.
5. Bind the quilt. *Party Whirl* has a 1" finished binding. Refer to Quilting Basics on page 87 for instructions.

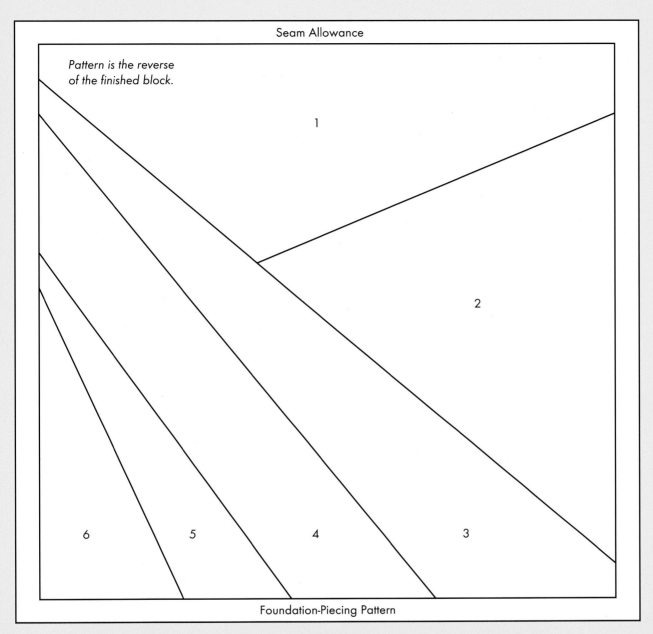

Seam Allowance

Pattern is the reverse
of the finished block.

1

2

6 5 4 3

Foundation-Piecing Pattern

Make 96

Garden Patch

By Theresa Eisinger

Originally designed as a border for a "gardening rabbit" fabric panel, these vegetable blocks were instead made into a thank-you quilt for the designer's sons' preschool teacher. The designer notes that the teacher is a wonderful woman who planted the first seeds of learning in many children's hearts.

Designed by Theresa Eisinger. Made by Maria Reardon Capp.

MATERIALS AND CUTTING

Quilt Size:		23" x 30"
Requirements are based on 42" fabric width.		
Borders include 2" extra length plus seam allowances.		
Read all instructions before cutting.		
Materials	Yards	Cutting
Green Print	¼	
inner borders (sides)		2 at 1½" x 28½
inner borders (top/bottom)		2 at 1½" x 23½"
Brown Print	¼	
outer borders (sides)		2 at 1½" x 30½"
outer borders (top/bottom)		2 at 1½" x 25½"
Red Print	¼	
binding		3 strips 2¼" x 42"
Assorted Fabric Scraps		
Nine-Patches*		63 A patches
setting strips*		57 A patches
vegetable blocks patches		3 B, 6 C, 6 D, 4 E, 4 F patches
Backing	1	
backing		1 panel 25" x 32"
sleeve		9" x 23"
Batting		4" longer and wider than quilt top

Supplies: Embroidery floss and metallic thread (optional)
* Refer to the Nine-Patch and setting-strip illustrations for value and color placements of the A patches.

GETTING STARTED

Wash and press fabrics. Cut the patches and other pieces as listed in the materials and cutting box. Refer to page 87 for Quilting Basics.

MAKING THE BLOCKS

1. Trace or photocopy four tomato tops, four tomato bottoms, five watermelons, four corn section 1, four corn section 2, two beet tops, two beet bottoms, five radish tops, five radish bottoms, six carrot and onion tops, three onion bottoms, and three carrot bottoms.

2. Foundation-piece the fabric units in numerical order. All the vegetable blocks are sewn in two sections and then joined. The watermelon block is sewn in one section.

3. Make four tomato tops, four tomato bottoms, five watermelons, four corn section 1, four corn section 2, two beet tops, two beet bottoms, five radish tops, five radish bottoms, six carrot and onion tops, three onion bottoms, and three carrot bottoms. Join the sections as needed to complete the blocks.

Fabric Tips

- Fabrics close to nature's own color scheme were chosen for *Garden Patch*. Using different textures and values of lights and darks helped differentiate fabrics of the same color.

- Cut the A–F patches from scrap fabrics and set them aside before beginning foundation-piecing.

ASSEMBLING THE QUILT TOP

1. Join the A patches to make the Nine-Patch units and setting strips, referring to illustrations for color and value placement and making the number of Nine-Patch units and setting strips indicated.

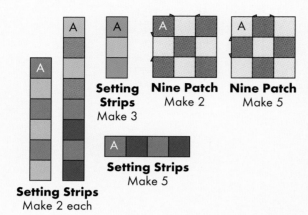

Setting Strips
Make 2 each

Setting Strips
Make 3

Nine Patch
Make 2

Nine Patch
Make 5

Setting Strips
Make 5

2. Arrange the blocks, Nine-Patch units, setting strips, and B–F patches as shown in quilt assembly. Join them into units; then join the units.

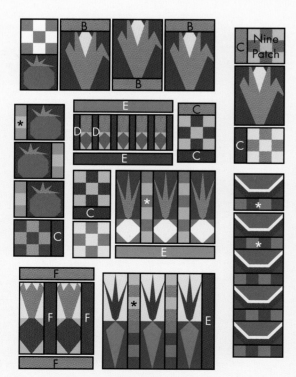

* = Setting Strip   **Quilt Assembly**

3. Press seam allowances away from the foundation-pieced blocks.

4. Sew the inner borders to the sides of the quilt and trim. Sew the inner borders to the top and bottom and trim. Press the seam allowances toward the borders.

5. Sew the outer borders to the sides of the quilt and trim. Sew the outer borders to the top and bottom and trim. Press the seam allowances toward the borders.

6. Remove the paper.

QUILTING AND FINISHING

1. If desired, embroider garden visitors and a metallic-thread spider web on the quilt top, referring to photo for placement.

2. Layer the quilt backing, batting, and top.

3. Baste.

4. Quilt the blocks and setting patches in-the-ditch, referring to quilting placement.

5. Trim quilt backing and batting even with the quilt top.

6. Join 2¼"-wide strips end to end to make the binding.

7. Bind the quilt.

8. Sew a sleeve to the backing for display purposes.

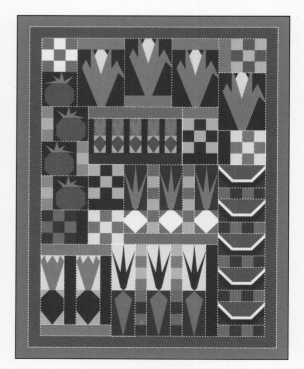

Quilting Placement

Tomato Bottom

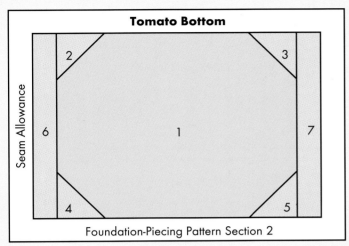

Seam Allowance

2   3

6   1   7

4   5

Foundation-Piecing Pattern Section 2

Make 4

Tomato Top

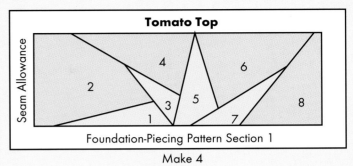

Seam Allowance

2   4   5   6   8

3   1   7

Foundation-Piecing Pattern Section 1

Make 4

Patterns are the reverse of the finished block.

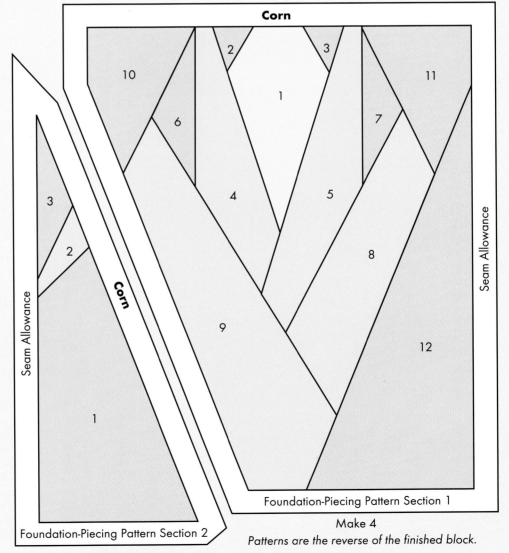

Corn

10   2   3   11

6   1   7

4   5

8

9   12

Seam Allowance

Seam Allowance

Foundation-Piecing Pattern Section 1

Make 4

Patterns are the reverse of the finished block.

Corn

3

2

1

Seam Allowance

Foundation-Piecing Pattern Section 2

Make 4

Watermelon

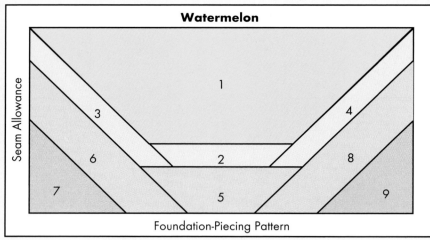

Foundation-Piecing Pattern

Make 5

Beet Top

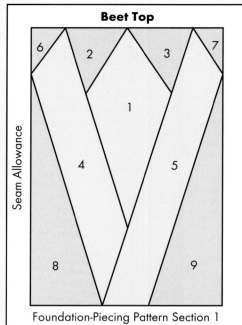

Foundation-Piecing Pattern Section 1

Make 2

Carrot and Onion Top

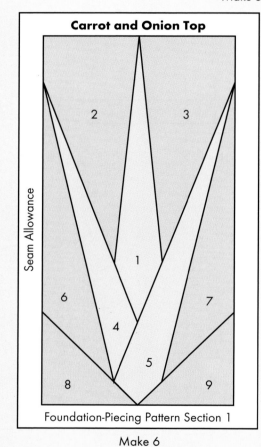

Foundation-Piecing Pattern Section 1

Make 6

Radish Top

Foundation-Piecing Pattern

Make 5

Radish Bottom

Foundation-Piecing Pattern

Make 5

Beet Bottom

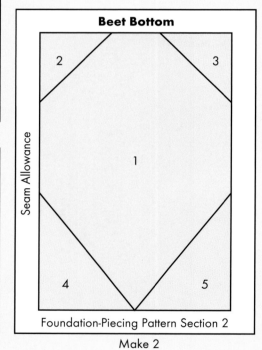

Foundation-Piecing Pattern Section 2

Make 2

Rotary Cutting

*Measurements include ¼"
seam allowance.
Align arrows
with lengthwise
or crosswise
grain of fabric.*

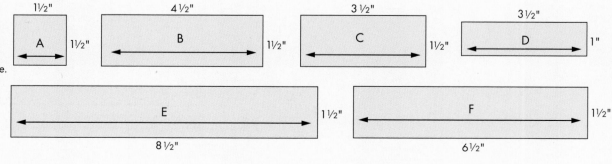

1½" · A · 1½"

4½" · B · 1½"

3½" · C · 1½"

3½" · D · 1"

E · 1½" · 8½"

F · 1½" · 6½"

 **Satin Stitch**  **Lazy-Daisy Stitch** **Couch Stitch**  **French Knot**  **Backstitch**

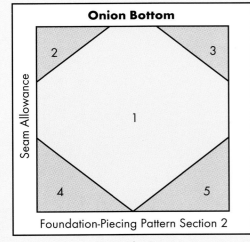

Onion Bottom

Seam Allowance

2   3

1

4   5

Foundation-Piecing Pattern Section 2

Make 3

Patterns are the reverse of the finished block.

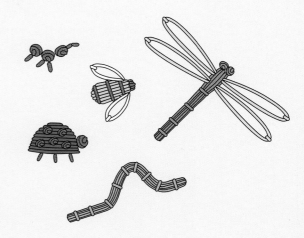

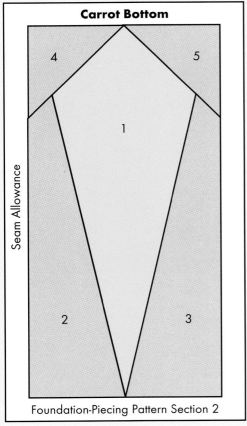

Carrot Bottom

Seam Allowance

4   5

1

2   3

Foundation-Piecing Pattern Section 2

Make 3

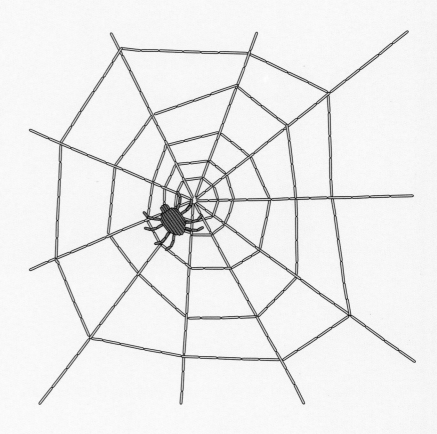

Secret Garden

By *Quiltmaker* Magazine Staff

t's easy to believe that fairies really do visit flower gardens when you look closely at *Secret Garden*, which includes an embroidered fairy in each block row. Delicate variations in color or value within each fabric create realistic-looking flowers and leaves.

Designed by the *Quiltmaker* Magazine staff. Made by Mickie Swall.

MATERIALS AND CUTTING

Block Sizes:		3 1/2" x 7", 3 1/2", 1 1/8" x 3 1/2"
Quilt Size:		46" x 41 5/8"
Requirements are based on 42" fabric width.		
Borders include 2" extra length plus seam allowances.		
Read all instructions before cutting.		
Materials	***Yards***	***Cutting***
Light Green Print	1/2	
sashes		5 strips 2 1/2" x 36"
Medium Green Print	1 3/8	
inner border (bottom)		1 at 2" x 43 1/2"
foundation piecing		leaves, stems
Green Print Scraps		leaves, stems
Blue, Lavender, and Pink Print Scraps		
flowers		30 at 5" x 6"
Light Blue Print	2 1/3	
inner border (top)		1 at 2" x 43 1/2"
inner borders (sides)		2 at 2" x 36"
A patches		2 at 7 1/2" x 5 1/8"
B patch		1 at 7 1/2" x 9 3/4"
Lavender Print	1 1/2	
outer borders (sides)		2 at 3" x 39"
outer borders (top/bottom)		2 at 3" x 48 1/2"
Purple Print	1/2	
binding		6 strips 2 1/4" x 34"
Yellow solid	3/8	flowers
Backing	2 3/4	
backing		2 panels 26" x 46"
sleeve		9" x 46"
Batting		4" longer and wider than quilt top

Supplies: Embroidery floss in flesh-tone, yellow, blue, and pink, template plastic

GETTING STARTED

Wash and press fabrics. Cut the patches and other pieces as listed in the materials and cutting box. Refer to page 87 for Quilting Basics.

MAKING THE BLOCKS

1. Trace or photocopy four U blocks, thirteen V blocks, thirteen W blocks, thirty-two X blocks, eleven Y blocks, and eleven Z blocks.
2. Foundation-piece the fabric units in numerical order.
3. Make four U blocks, thirteen V blocks, thirteen W blocks, thirty-two X blocks, eleven Y blocks, and eleven Z blocks.

ASSEMBLING THE QUILT TOP

1. Join the blocks and patches to make vertical rows, referring to the row assembly for placement.

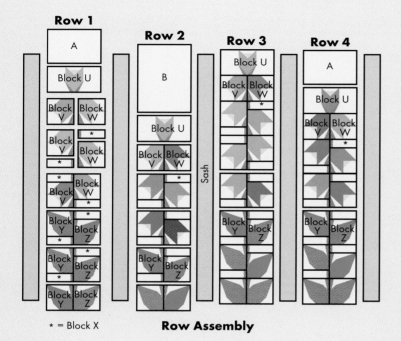

Row 1

Row 2

Row 3

Row 4

* = Block X

Row Assembly

2. Make one of each row.

3. Press the seam allowances open between the blocks.

4. Sew a sash to row 3 and press seam allowances toward the sash. Trim the sash even with the block row. Measure the length of the sewn sash and trim the remaining four sashes to match. Working from the center outward, join the rows and sashes in the order shown, easing the rows to fit if necessary.

5. Press the seam allowances toward the sashes.

6. Sew the inner borders to the sides of the quilt and trim. Sew the inner borders to the top and bottom and trim. Press the seam allowances toward the borders.

7. Sew the outer borders to the sides of the quilt and trim. Sew the outer borders to the top and bottom and trim. Press the seam allowances toward the borders.

8. Remove the paper.

QUILTING AND FINISHING

1. Trace the outline of the fairy and transfer four fairies to the quilt, referring to photo for placement.

2. Satin stitch the fairies' arms, legs, and faces, using two strands of flesh-tone embroidery floss. Embroider the remainder of each fairy, using single strands of rayon or cotton floss in the colors shown. Outline stitch the wings and Backstitch the dresses and hats. Decorate each dress and hat with Lazy-Daisy stitches and French knots. Embroider the motifs in the wings, using the Single stitch.

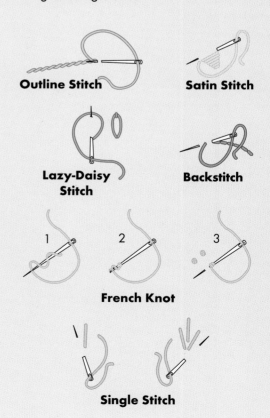

Outline Stitch

Satin Stitch

Lazy-Daisy Stitch

Backstitch

1 2 3

French Knot

Single Stitch

3. Trace the green, blue, and purple butterfly ballet quilting motifs and positioning guides onto see-through template plastic. Cut out the three shapes.

4. Fold each sash in half lengthwise and crosswise and crease lightly. Matching guidelines to the creases, trace the green motif in the center of the first sash. Flip the template, match the guideline, and mark another motif on either side of the first one. Continue flipping and marking to trace nine motifs in the sash. Repeat for remaining sashes, alternating the orientation of the first marked motif as shown in quilting placement.

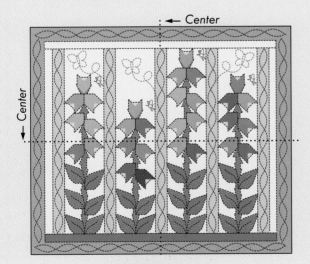

Quilting Placement

5. Fold each border in half lengthwise and crosswise and crease lightly. Matching guidelines to the creases, trace the green motif in the center

of the first border. Flip the template, match the guideline, and mark another motif on either side of the first one. Continue flipping and marking to fill the border. Repeat for remaining borders, referring to the quilting placement.

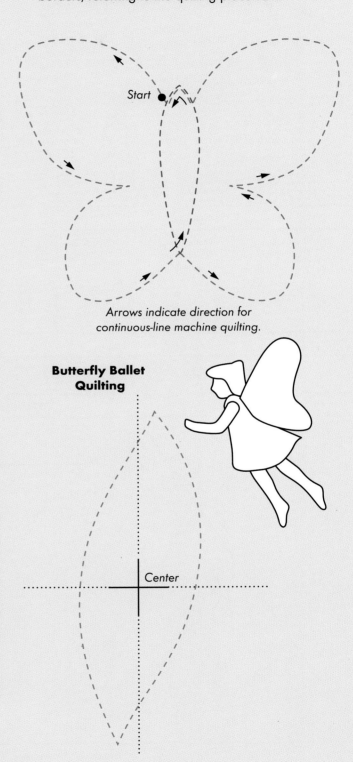

Arrows indicate direction for continuous-line machine quilting.

Butterfly Ballet Quilting

6. Trace the butterfly's wings and then the body in three of the rows, referring to the quilting placement. Randomly mark butterfly paths and mark a vein in each leaf.

7. Layer the quilt backing, batting, and top.

8. Baste.

9. Quilt in-the-ditch around the flowers, leaves, stems, sashes, and borders. Quilt the marked lines.

10. Trim quilt backing and batting even with the quilt top.

11. Join 2¼"-wide strips end to end to make the binding.

12. Bind the quilt.

13. Sew a sleeve to the backing for display purposes.

CHANGE THE MOOD

Reversing the values of the background and flower gives the appearance of a garden in the moonlight. Each white flower contains a hint of color, adding subtle interest. For a lovely small wall hanging, add a border to a single row from *Secret Garden*.

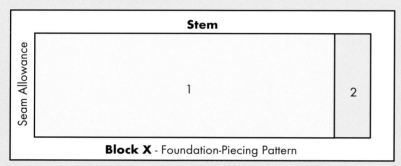

Block X - Foundation-Piecing Pattern

Make 32

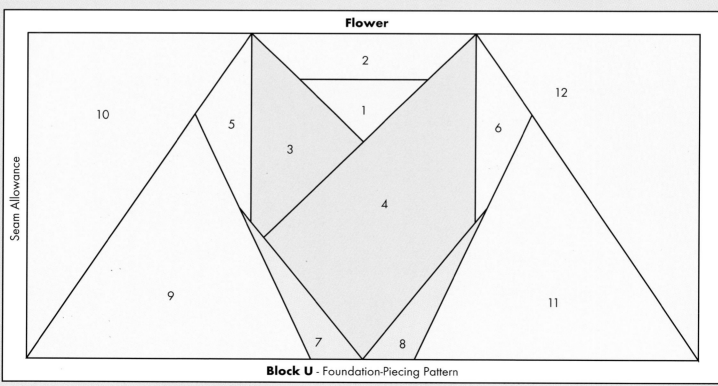

Block U - Foundation-Piecing Pattern

Patterns are the reverse of the finished block.

Make 4

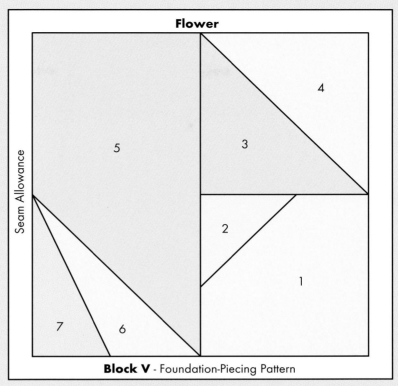

Flower

Seam Allowance

5

4

3

2

1

7 6

Block V - Foundation-Piecing Pattern

Make 13

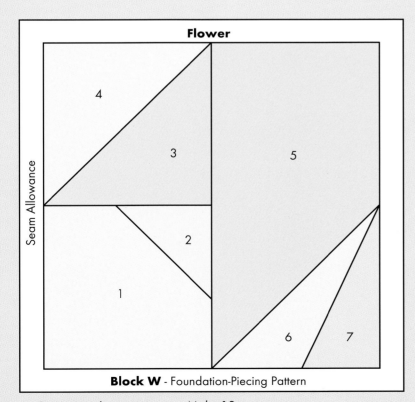

Flower

Seam Allowance

4

3

5

2

1

6 7

Block W - Foundation-Piecing Pattern

*Patterns are the reverse
of the finished block.*

Make 13

Rotary Cutting
*Measurements include ¼ " seam allowance.
Align arrows with lengthwise or
crosswise grain of fabric.*

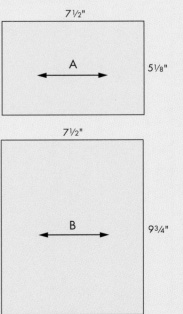

7½"

A

5⅛"

7½"

B

9¾"

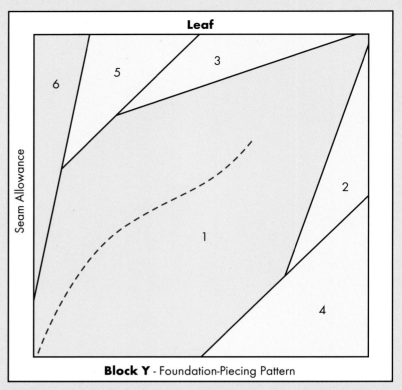

Leaf

Seam Allowance

Block Y - Foundation-Piecing Pattern

*Patterns are the reverse
of the finished block.*

Make 11

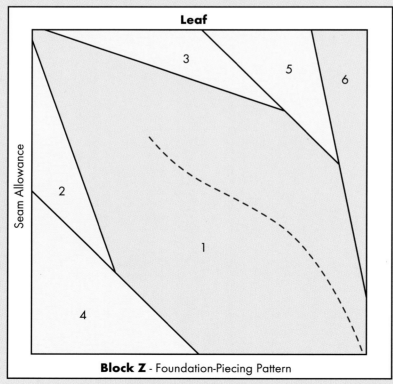

Leaf

Seam Allowance

Block Z - Foundation-Piecing Pattern

Make 11

Wee Houses

INTERMEDIATE ▶ ▶   By Brenda Groelz

This delightful little house pattern, appropriately titled *Wee Houses,* is for anyone who wants to do an enjoyable project that includes paper-foundation piecing. The block is given in two sizes, small and smaller! The quilt shown is made using the smaller block size.

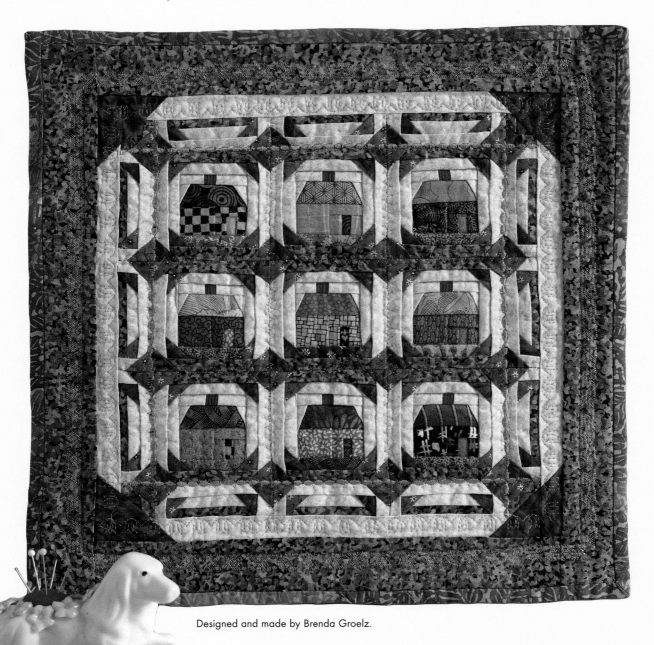

Designed and made by Brenda Groelz.

MATERIALS AND CUTTING

Block Sizes:		2½"	[5"]	
Quilt Sizes: Smaller (shown), [Small]			12½"	[25"]

Requirements are based on 42" fabric width.

Borders include 2" extra length plus seam allowances.

Read all instructions before cutting.

Materials	Yards	Cutting	Materials	Yards	Cutting
Smaller Quilt			**Small Quilt**		
Light Fabric	¼	background patches	**Light Fabric**	5/8	background patches
Red Scraps			**Red Scraps**		
chimneys		9 at ¾" x 8"	chimneys		9 at 1" x 10"
Assorted Scraps		remaining patches	**Assorted Scraps**		remaining patches
Blue Print	¼		**Blue Print**	½	
borders		4 at 1¾" x 11½"	borders		4 at 3" x 20½"
Blue/Red Print	¼		**Blue/Red Print**	3/8	
binding		4 strips 2¼" x 15½"	binding		4 strips 2¼" x 28"
Backing	¾	1 panel 18½" x 18½"	**Backing**	1	1 panel 31" x 31"
Batting		4" longer and wider	**Batting**		4" longer and wider
		than quilt top			than quilt top

Supplies: Metallic thread   Supplies: Metallic thread

Directions are for both the small quilt and the smaller quilt. Information that differs for the small quilt is shown in [ ].

GETTING STARTED

Wash and press fabrics. Cut the patches and other pieces as listed in the materials and cutting box. Refer to page 87 for Quilting Basics.

MAKING THE BLOCKS

1. Trace or photocopy nine 2½" [5"] house blocks, twelve 2½" [5"] border units, and four 2½" [5"] corner units.

2. Make nine chimney sections, sewing a ¾" x 8" [1" x 10"] strip of the chimney fabric between two 1¼" x 8" [1¾" x 10"] strips of the background fabric. Cut this band crosswise into nine ¾"-wide [1"-wide] segments.

3. Foundation-piece the fabric units in numerical order, using the chimney sections (from Step 2) for the #9 patches.

4. Make nine house blocks, twelve border units, and four corner units.

ASSEMBLING THE QUILT TOP

1. Arrange all the blocks and units in horizontal rows, referring to the partial quilt assembly.

2. Sew blocks and units in rows; then join the rows.

3. Sew a 1" x 8½" [1½" x 16½"] light border to each side, trimming the ends even with the angled corner units.

4. Sew an outer corner triangle A patch [AA patch] to each corner.

5. Sew 1¾"-wide [3"-wide] blue borders to the top and bottom of the quilt.

6. Sew 1¾"-wide [3"-wide] blue borders to the sides of the quilt.

7. Remove the paper.

QUILTING AND FINISHING

1. Layer the quilt backing, batting, and top.

2. Baste.

3. Quilt between the blocks using metallic thread and fancy machine-embroidery stitches.

4. Quilt around the doors, windows, and rooflines.

5. Trim quilt backing and batting even with the quilt top.

6. Join 2¼"-wide strips end to end to make the binding.

7. Bind the quilt.

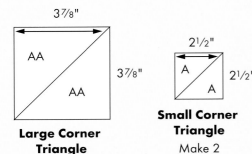

Large Corner Triangle
Make 2

Small Corner Triangle
Make 2

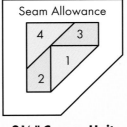

2½" Corner Unit
Foundation-Piecing Pattern
Make 4

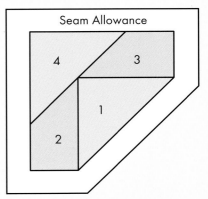

5" Corner Unit
Foundation-Piecing Pattern
Make 4

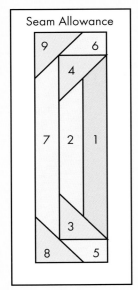

2½" Border Unit
Foundation-Piecing Pattern
Make 12

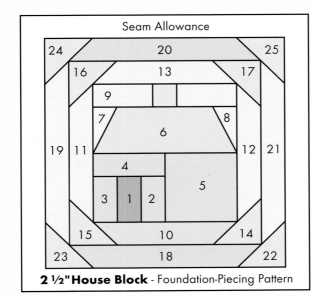

2½" House Block - Foundation-Piecing Pattern

Make 9

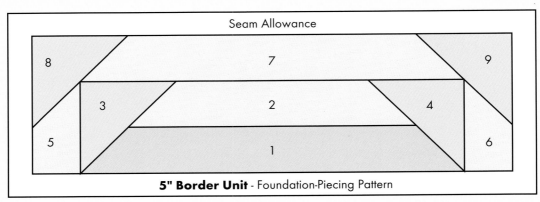

5" Border Unit - Foundation-Piecing Pattern

Make 12

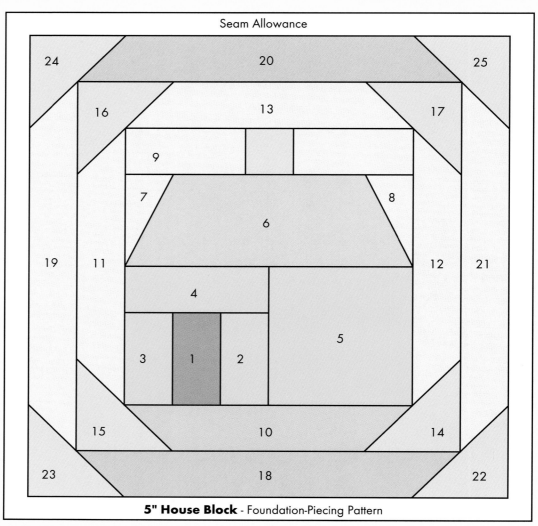

5" House Block - Foundation-Piecing Pattern

Make 9

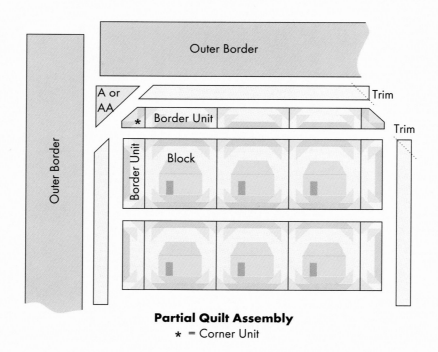

Partial Quilt Assembly

∗ = Corner Unit

Fireworks

By Kyoko Honda

A collection of old kimonos and a workshop with Chieko Shibata inspired Kyoko Honda of Toyota, Japan, to make this marvelous silk quilt. Further inspiration for color and print selection came from a fireworks display the designer enjoys each summer. A traditional Pineapple block provided the ideal pattern to create a design bursting with color and reminiscent of exploding fireworks against a night sky.

This quilt's maker hand-pieced her quilt blocks, but paper-foundation-piecing instructions have been included for those who prefer machine work for this part of the quiltmaking process. In addition, instructions are given for using a permanent foundation, which may be preferable to paper if using silk fabrics.

Designed and made by Kyoko Honda.

MATERIALS AND CUTTING

Block Size: 5¾"

Quilt Size: 81½" x 81½"

Requirements are based on 42" fabric width.

Borders include 2" extra length plus seam allowances.

Read all instructions before cutting.

Materials	Yards	Cutting
Muslin or Interfacing (optional)	4½	144 6¼" squares
Border Print	2½	
borders		4 at 6¾" x 84"
binding		9 strips 2¼" x 42"
Black/Yellow Print	1¾	144 each #1, 18, 19 patches
Dark Scraps	3	144 each #2, 3, 6, 7, 10, 11, 14, 15 patches
Bright Print Scraps	7	144 each #4, 5, 8, 9, 12, 13, 16, 17 patches
Backing	5	2 panels 43" x 85"
Batting		4" longer and wider than quilt top

TIP

Fabric Tips

- The following amounts of bright prints will be needed for the blocks. For each block: 42" x 1¾" (or fat eighth); for each 2-block unit: 42" x 2¾" (or fat eighth); for each 3-block unit: 42" x 4½" (or fat eighth); for each 4-block unit: 42" x 5½" (or fat quarter). In addition, ⅞ yard of one print will be needed for the twenty blocks that are placed around the center of the quilt.

- If using silk fabric, a muslin or nonwoven interfacing, rather than paper, may be used for the foundations. The fabric foundations will remain as part of the blocks. In addition, the fabric foundations will give body to the silk.

GETTING STARTED

Wash and press fabrics. Cut the patches and other pieces as listed in the materials and cutting box. Refer to page 87 for Quilting Basics.

MAKING THE BLOCKS

1. Trace or photocopy 144 complete blocks if using paper. If using a muslin or non-woven interfacing for foundation, use a light table and mark the lines with a pencil or permanent pen on squares.

2. Foundation-piece the fabric units in numerical order.

3. Make four 1-block units, eight 2-block units, twelve 3-block units, and seventeen 4-block units. In addition, make twenty 1-block units from one print. Keep these twenty 1-block units separate.

4. If using paper, remove it.

1-Block
Make 4
Also make 20
from one print

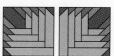

2-Block Unit
Make 8

3-Block Unit
Make 12

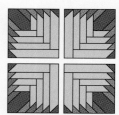

4-Block Unit
Make 17

ASSEMBLING THE QUILT TOP

1. Position the units in twelve horizontal rows, referring to the quilt assembly and being careful to keep the units made from the same fabrics together to form the design.
2. Join the units in rows; then join the rows.
3. Sew the borders to each side, mitering the corners and trimming the excess seam allowances.

QUILTING AND FINISHING

1. Mark twelve motifs in each border and one in each corner, matching dots.

2. Layer the quilt backing, batting, and top.
3. Baste.
4. Quilt curved lines around the center of the quilt and diagonal lines radiating from the curved lines to the edges of the border, referring to quilt assembly and photo.
5. Quilt the border as marked.
6. Trim quilt backing and batting even with the quilt top.
7. Join 2¼"-wide strips end to end to make the binding.
8. Bind the quilt.

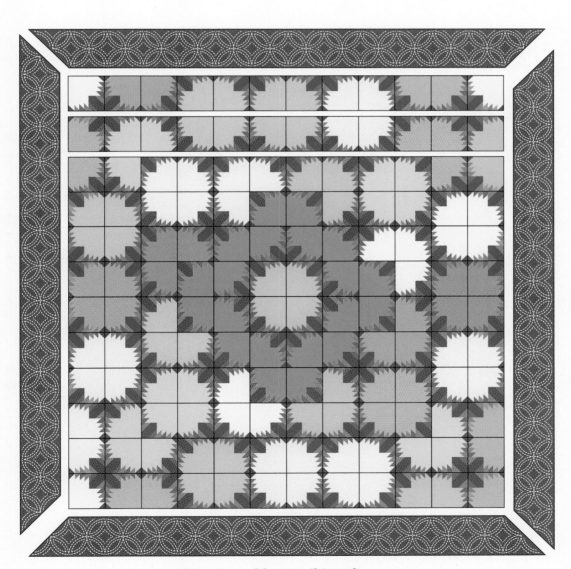

Quilting Assembly & Quilting Placement

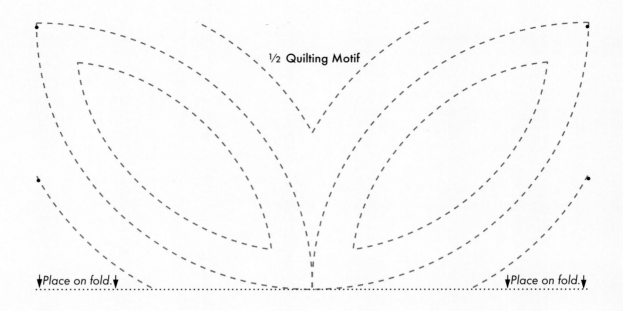

½ **Quilting Motif**

↓*Place on fold.*↓ ↓*Place on fold.*↓

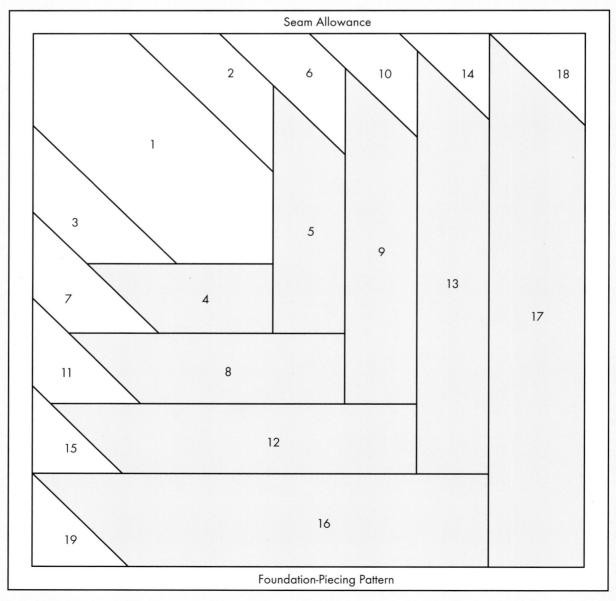

Seam Allowance

Foundation-Piecing Pattern

Pineapple Slices

INTERMEDIATE ▶ ▶

By Kathy Mitchell

When Kathy Mitchell of Carmichael, California, wanted to start a new quilt, she was inspired by the book *Pineapple Passion,* by Lynda Milligan and Nancy Smith, owners of Possibilities. Kathy particularly liked the Four-Patch blocks in the sashing, and added her own design twist when she carried the blocks through to the border.

Exhibited at the American Quilters' Society show in Paducah, Kentucky, this quilt was constructed using paper-foundation-piecing methods to ensure a precisely pieced 10" block.

Designed and made by Kathy Mitchell.

MATERIALS AND CUTTING

Materials	Yards	Cutting
Block Size:		10"
Quilt Size:		86" x 98"

Requirements are based on 42" fabric width.

Borders are the exact length required plus seam allowances.

Read all instructions before cutting.

Materials	Yards	Cutting
White	6½	
B patches		97 at 2½" x 10½"
inner borders (sides)		2 at 2½" x 86½"
inner borders (top/bottom)		2 at 2½" x 78½"
outer borders (sides)		2 at 2½" x 94½"
outer borders (top/bottom)		2 at 2½" x 86½"
straight-grain strips		64 strips 1¾" x 40"
Scrap Prints	7½	1,080 A patches; 168 #10 patches
straight-grain strips		1¾"-wide (cut as needed)
binding		10 strips 2¼" x 42"
Backing	7⅞	3 panels 35" x 90"
Batting		4" longer and wider than quilt top

Fabric Tip

- If using scraps, a minimum piece of 9" x 14" or a fat ⅛ yard of each color within each Pineapple block will be needed.

GETTING STARTED

Wash and press fabrics. Cut the patches and other pieces as listed in the materials and cutting box. Refer to page 87 for Quilting Basics.

MAKING THE BLOCKS

1. Trace or photocopy forty-two complete blocks. Make a template for the #10 patch, adding a generous seam allowance.

2. Using four A squares cut from two different fabrics for each unit, make forty-two Four-Patch units for the block centers (# 1 patch).

3. On the back side of the foundation paper, align the edges of a Four-Patch unit, right side up, with the dashed lines. Pin block in place to prevent shifting.

4. On the back side of the paper foundation, place a white straight-grain strip on top of #1 patch, placing right sides of fabric together and keeping raw edges even. Hold the fabric in place and turn the paper over. Re-pin the fabrics from the drawn side and remove the pin (from Step 3) from the fabric side. Using short, straight stitches, sew along the solid line.

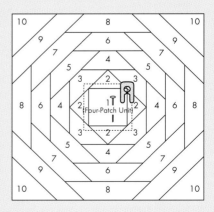

5. Trim the end of the strip even with the Four-Patch unit.

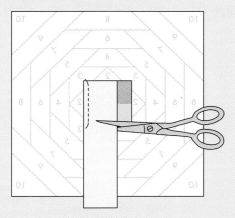

6. Press the strip open.
7. Sew remaining #2 patches around the center.

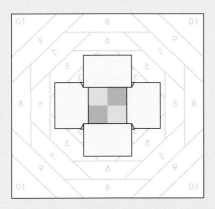

8. Using a block-color fabric, cut a strip 1¾" wide. Hold the pattern to the light and align this strip ¼" beyond the seam line for a #3 patch, placing right sides of fabric together. Sew on the paper side along the solid line and trim strip at end of sewing. Trim the triangular

excess from the #2 patches, using the edge of the strip as a guide.

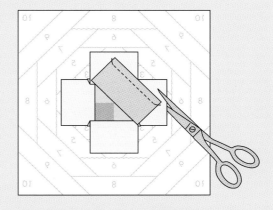

9. Sew all the #3 patches, alternating colors.
10. Continue foundation piecing the fabric units in numerical order, ending with a #10 patch in each corner.
11. Trim the outside edges of the blocks, leaving a ¼" seam allowance.
12. Make forty-two blocks.
13. Remove the paper.

ASSEMBLING THE QUILT TOP

1. Place the blocks on a large, flat surface, arranging as needed to achieve desired color placement.
2. Each Four-Patch unit setting square is made with A squares that match the adjoining blocks. Make fifty-six setting squares in the appropriate fabrics.

Four-Patch Unit
Make 172 for the borders
Make 42 for block centers
Make 56 for setting squares

3. Join the blocks, B sashing strips, and Four-Patch setting squares in seven rows of six blocks, referring to partial quilt assembly.

4. Make 172 Four-Patch units for the borders. Set aside.

5. Sew the inner borders to the sides of the quilt. Sew the inner borders to the top and bottom. Press the seam allowances toward the borders.

6. Sew forty-five Four-Patch units together to make one Four-Patch side border. Repeat for opposite Four-Patch side border. Sew Four-Patch side borders to quilt.

7. Sew forty-one Four-Patch units together to make the top Four-Patch border. Repeat for bottom border. Sew Four-Patch top and bottom borders to quilt. Press the seam allowances toward the borders.

8. Sew the outer borders to the sides of the quilt. Sew the outer borders to the top and bottom. Press the seam allowances toward the borders.

QUILTING AND FINISHING

1. Layer the quilt backing, batting, and top.
2. Baste.
3. Stipple-quilt over all of the white patches.
4. Trim quilt backing and batting even with the quilt top.
5. Join 2¼"-wide strips end to end to make the binding.
6. Bind the quilt.

Changing the fabric used can completely alter the look of a quilt. Here, substituting a black print fabric for the white, and dark and bright colors in place of the lighter prints, gives these Pineapple blocks a completely different appearance than those used by the designer to create *Pineapple Slices*.

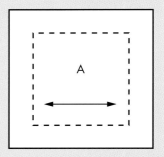

Rotary Cutting
Measurements include ¼" seam allowance.
Align arrows with lengthwise or
crosswise grain of fabric.

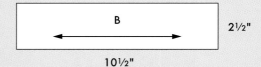

2½"

10½"

* = Four-Patch Unit

Partial Quilt Assembly

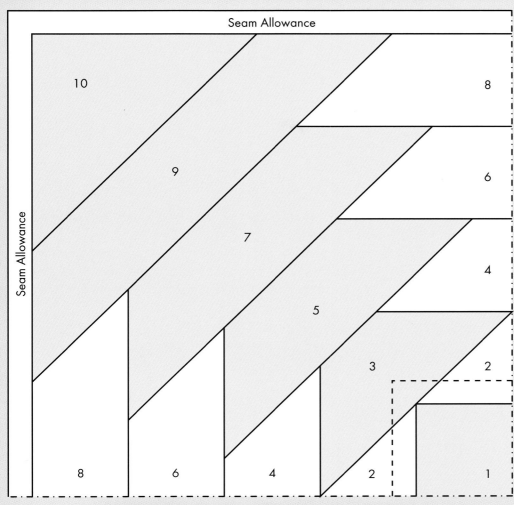

Seam Allowance

Seam Allowance

10

9

8

7

6

5

4

3

2

8   6   4   2   1

Pineapple Block - Foundation-Piecing Pattern - Quadrant

Trace or photocopy 4 quadrants and tape or glue together to make one Pineapple block pattern.

Make 42 complete block patterns.

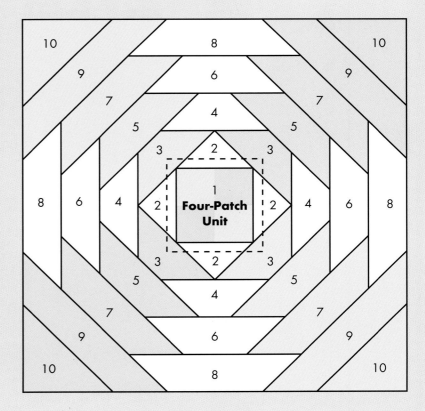

10   8   10
9   6   9
7   4   7
5   5
3   2   3
2
1
8 6 4 2 Four-Patch 2 4 6 8
Unit
3   2   3
5   5
4
7   7
9   6   9
10   8   10

Sunflowers

INTERMEDIATE ▶▶

By Nancy Breland

The tall, vertical form of the sunflower provided the ideal inspiration for strippy sets for Nancy Breland of Pennington, New Jersey. The Wheel of Fortune block was used to form the flowers.

Determining the block to use was perhaps the easiest part of creating these large buds. Nancy notes that it was quite a challenge to find a good selection of fabrics in the colors she sought for the flower centers and petals. Her efforts created this colorful quilt with sunflowers that seem to reach toward the sky.

Designed and made by Nancy Breland.

Block Size:		7¼" x 10¼"
Quilt Size:		64" x 81½"

Requirements are based on 42" fabric width.

Borders are the exact length required plus seam allowances.

Read all instructions before cutting.

Materials	Yards	Cutting
White/Cream Solids	¾	192 B patches
Tan Scraps	2½	192 B, 192 C, 96 D, 24 F, 24 Fr, 24 G, 24 Gr,
		48 H patches
Yellow Floral	2	
inner borders (sides)		2 at 5½" x 64"
inner borders (top/bottom)		2 at 5½" x 56½"
sashes		3 at 3½" x 64"
Orange Print	½	24 A patches
Green Print	2¼	
outer borders (sides)		2 at 4½" x 74"
outer borders (top/bottom)		2 at 4½" x 64½"
sashes		8 at 1½" x 62"
sashes		8 at 1½" x 93¾"
Orange Solid	1¼	
binding		8 strips 2¼" x 42"
narrow folded strips		8 strips ¾" x 64" (cut crosswise and pieced)
		8 strips ¾" x 93¾"
Red/Orange Scraps	1½	384 B patches
Green Scraps	¾	24 E, 24 Er, 24 I patches
Backing	5	2 panels 35" x 86" each
Batting		4" longer and wider than quilt top

GETTING STARTED

Wash and press fabrics. Cut the patches and other pieces as listed in the materials and cutting box. Refer to page 87 for Quilting Basics.

MAKING THE BLOCKS

1. Trace or photocopy twenty-four complete blocks. (Eight flower units are required for each block.)
2. Foundation-piece the fabric units in numerical order, noting that the cream fabric is always used in the #5 patch of the flower unit.
3. Make 192 flower units, twenty-four leaf unit 1, and twenty-four leaf unit 2.
4. Remove the paper.
5. Referring to the block assembly, sew a flower unit to one edge of the octagon, sewing a partial seam, as indicated by the *. Moving in a counterclockwise direction, sew a second flower unit to the octagon. Continue in a counterclockwise direction, sewing all eight flower units to the octagon. Complete the first seam.

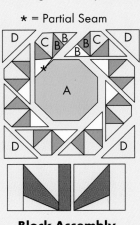

* = Partial Seam

Block Assembly
Make 24

6. Make twenty-four flowers.

7. Sew a leaf unit 1 to a leaf unit 2 to make one complete leaf.

8. Make twenty-four leaves.

9. Sew a leaf to the bottom of each flower to complete the blocks.

ASSEMBLING THE QUILT TOP

1. Join the blocks in four vertical rows of six blocks each, as shown in the partial quilt assembly.

2. Sew a long green sash to the long edges of each block row. Sew short green sashes to the top and bottom of each block row.

3. Fold the ¾"-wide orange strips in half lengthwise, right sides out, and press. Align a long folded orange strip with the long side of a green sash, keeping raw edges even. Baste ⅛" from raw edge. Repeat for the opposite side. Align a short orange strip at the top and bottom and baste. Refer to the partial quilt assembly detail. Repeat for all rows.

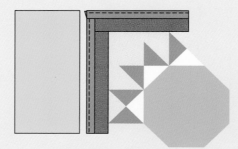

Partial Quilt Assembly Detail

4. Sew the four block rows alternately with the three yellow floral sashes. The orange folded strips will be caught in the seams.

5. Sew the long floral print borders to the sides. Press seam allowances toward the floral print borders so that the orange strips lie on top of the green borders. Sew the short floral print borders to the top and bottom and press as before. Trim.

6. Sew the long green borders to the sides and short green borders to the top and bottom and trim.

Partial Quilt Assembly

QUILTING AND FINISHING

1. Mark the leaf motif in the green borders, matching dots to form a continuous leaf-quilting pattern. Reduce the leaf motif by 75% on a photocopy machine and mark it in the yellow sashes. Mark the sun-quilting motif in the top left A patch, if desired.

2. Layer the quilt backing, batting, and top.

3. Baste.

4. Quilt in-the-ditch around the patches in the flower blocks and along the seams of the sashes and borders.

5. Quilt the leaf pattern in the yellow sashes.

6. Machine quilt concentric curves and rays in the yellow floral borders.

7. Quilt the leaves in the border.

8. Quilt the sun face in the A patch, if desired.

9. Trim quilt backing and batting even with the quilt top.

10. Join 2¼"-wide strips end to end to make the binding.

11. Bind the quilt.

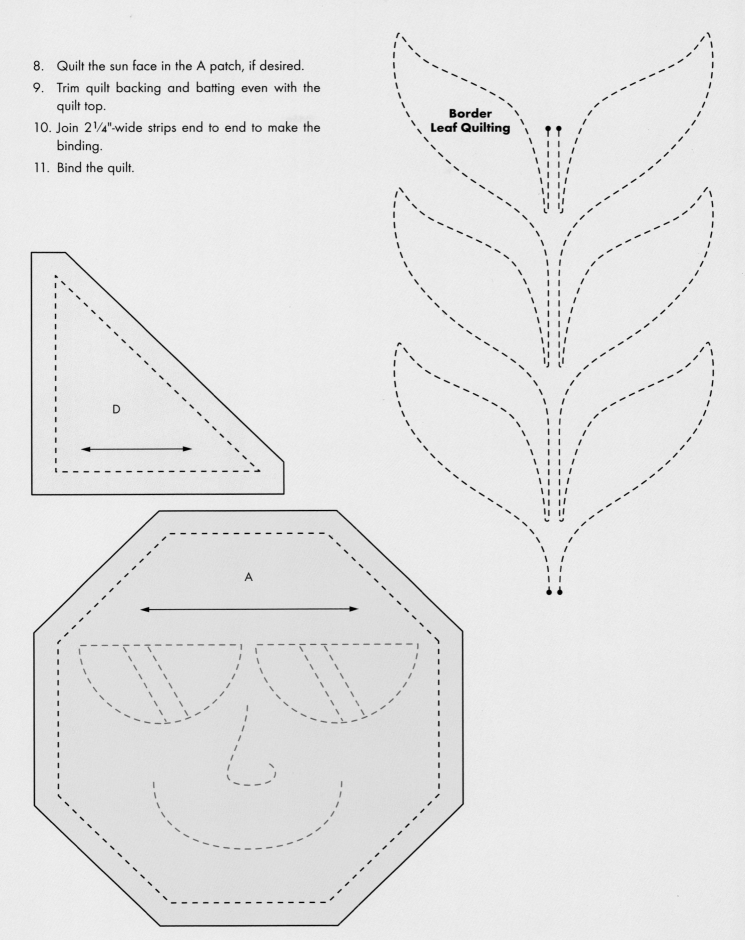

Border Leaf Quilting

D

A

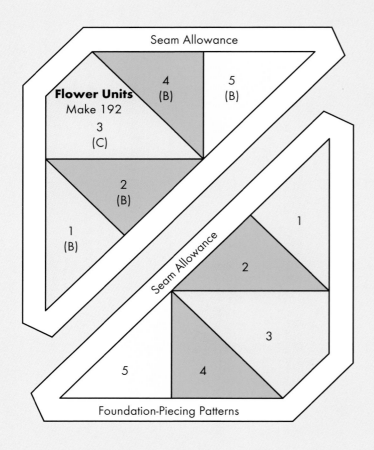

Flower Units
Make 192

Seam Allowance

4
(B)

5
(B)

3
(C)

2
(B)

1
(B)

Seam Allowance

1

2

3

5

4

Foundation-Piecing Patterns

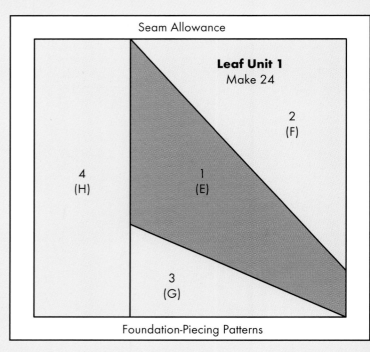

Seam Allowance

Leaf Unit 1
Make 24

2
(F)

4
(H)

1
(E)

3
(G)

Foundation-Piecing Patterns

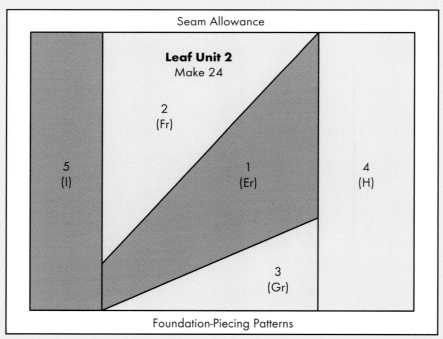

Seam Allowance

Leaf Unit 2
Make 24

2
(Fr)

5
(I)

1
(Er)

4
(H)

3
(Gr)

Foundation-Piecing Patterns

Letters indicate patches needed. Numbers indicate the order of piecing patches on paper foundations. Paper-foundation units are the reverse of the finished block.

Pink Dogwood

INTERMEDIATE ▶ ▶

By Nancy Breland

Nancy Breland, of Pennington, New Jersey, created *Pink Dogwood* using a large-print fabric she found irresistible. The strippy set design of this quilt provided an ideal use for substantial amounts of the fabric, which reminded Nancy of dogwood blossoms, leaves, and buds. She designed the flower blocks to go with the fabric. Narrow folded strips of green inserted in some of the seams add a delicate touch of color. This quilt and *Sunflowers,* which appears on page 52 and was also designed by Nancy, are a testament to how much block design, fabric color, and placement can change the appearance of a design concept.

Designed and made by Nancy Breland.

MATERIALS AND CUTTING

Block Size:		9"
Quilt Size:		73¼" x 86¼"

Requirements are based on 42" fabric width.

Borders are the exact length required plus seam allowances.

Read all instructions before cutting.

Materials	Yards	Cutting
Cream Print	2½	backgrounds
Tan Print	1	leaf units
		84 strips 1¼" x 5"
Floral Print	2	
inner borders (sides)		2 at 5⅛" x 65½"
inner borders (top/bottom)		2 at 5⅝" x 62¾"
sashes		3 at 3½" x 65½"
Yellow Print	⅛	28 block centers
Rose Print	¾	
sashes		8 at 1½" x 63½" (cut crosswise and pieced)
sashes		8 at 1½" x 11½"
Rose Scraps	1¾	pieced blocks and borders
Wine Print	⅜	pieced blocks
Green Print	¾	
narrow borders (sides)		2 at 1½" x 75¾" (cut crosswise and pieced)
narrow borders (top/bottom)		2 at 1½" x 64¾" (cut crosswise and pieced)
narrow folded strips		8 strips ¾" x 65½" (cut crosswise and pieced)
narrow folded strips		8 strips ¾" x 11½"
Green Scraps	1½	block and border leaves
Binding	¾	9 strips 2¼" x 42"
Backing	5⅜	2 panels 38" x 90"
Batting		4" longer and wider than quilt top

GETTING STARTED

Wash and press fabrics. Cut the patches and other pieces as listed in the materials and cutting box. Refer to page 87 for Quilting Basics.

MAKING THE BLOCKS

1. Trace or photocopy twenty-eight unit A, fifty-six unit B, fifty-six unit C, fifty-six unit D, and fifty-six unit E.

2. Foundation-piece the fabric units in numerical order.

3. Make twenty-eight unit A, fifty-six unit B, fifty-six unit C, fifty-six unit D, and fifty-six unit E.

4. Remove the paper.

5. Join the units to make twenty-eight Dogwood blocks, referring to Dogwood block piecing.

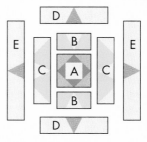

**Dogwood
Block Piecing**

ASSEMBLING THE QUILT TOP

1. Join seven Dogwood blocks end to end to make a vertical row, referring to the partial quilt assembly. Make four rows.

2. Sew a long rose sash to the long edges of each block row. Sew short rose sashes to the top and bottom of each block row.

3. Fold the ¾"-wide green strips in half lengthwise, right sides out, and press. Align a long folded green strip with the long side of a rose sash, keeping raw edges even. Baste ⅛" from raw edge. Repeat for the opposite side. Align a short green strip at the top and bottom and baste. Refer to the detail in the partial quilt assembly. Repeat for all rows.

4. Sew the four block rows alternately with the three floral print sashes. The green folded strips will be caught in the seams.

5. Sew the long floral print borders to the sides. Press seam allowances toward the floral print borders so that the green strips lie on top of the rose borders. Sew the short floral print borders to the top and bottom and press as before.

6. Sew long green borders to the sides and short green borders to the top and bottom.

7. Use the paper-foundation piecing method using freezer paper (see tip box below) to make eighty-eight border leaves and four corner flowers.

**Corner Flower
Block Piecing**

Border Leaf Block

8. Remove the paper.

9. Join twenty leaves alternately with nineteen 1¼" x 5" tan strips. Sew to the quilt top. Repeat for the quilt bottom. Join twenty-four leaves alternately with twenty-three tan strips. Sew a corner flower to each end. Sew to one side of quilt. Repeat for opposite side.

Piecing Tips

1. Trace the full-size pattern onto freezer paper. Mark grain-line arrows on patterns. Cut the paper patches apart to use as templates.

2. Iron each template to the wrong side of fabric. Cut fabric patches with a ¼" seam allowance on the sides of each patch that will be sewn to another patch in the unit. Cut the seam allowances for the outside edges of the unit ½" or more beyond the paper.

3. Foundation-piece the fabric units in numerical order, using the freezer paper to help align the patch to the foundation. Using this method will maintain the exact angle of the grain line, ensuring that the patch will cover the pattern. Trim the

unit, leaving a ¼" seam allowance all around. Remove the freezer paper and re-use.

QUILTING AND FINISHING

1. Layer the quilt backing, batting, and top.
2. Baste.
3. Quilt in-the-ditch around the patches.
4. Quilt around the printed motifs of the floral border.
5. Trim quilt backing and batting even with the quilt top.
6. Join 2¼"-wide strips end to end to make the binding.
7. Bind the quilt.

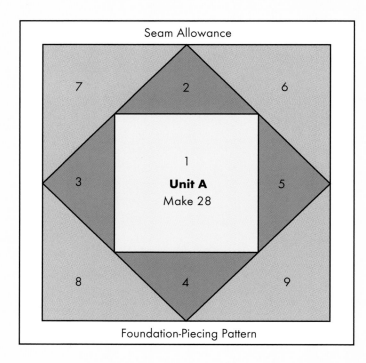

Seam Allowance

Unit A
Make 28

Foundation-Piecing Pattern

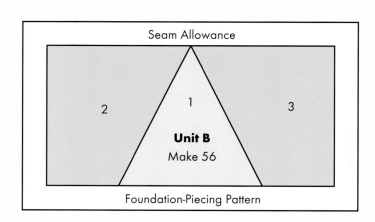

Seam Allowance

Unit B
Make 56

Foundation-Piecing Pattern

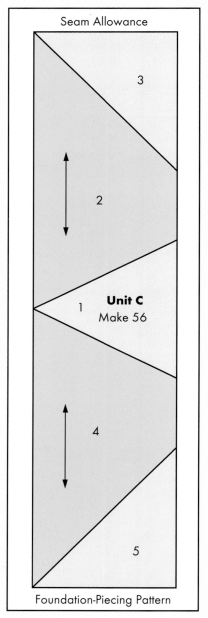

Seam Allowance

Unit C
Make 56

Foundation-Piecing Pattern

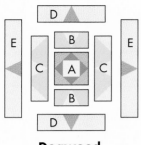

**Dogwood
Block Piecing**

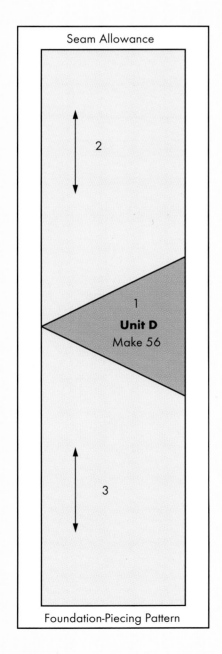

Seam Allowance

2

1

Unit D
Make 56

3

Foundation-Piecing Pattern

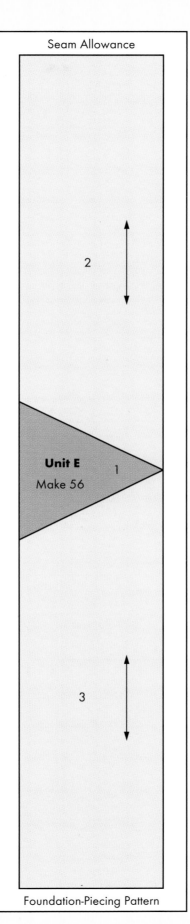

Seam Allowance

2

1

Unit E
Make 56

3

Foundation-Piecing Pattern

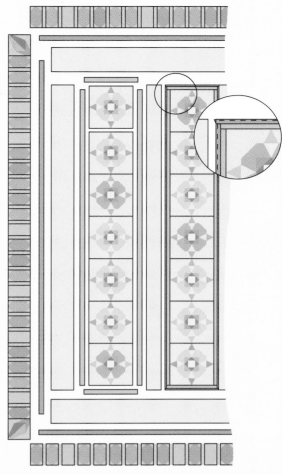

Partial Quilt Assembly

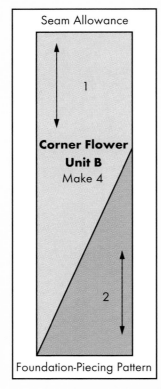

Seam Allowance

1

**Corner Flower
Unit B**
Make 4

2

Foundation-Piecing Pattern

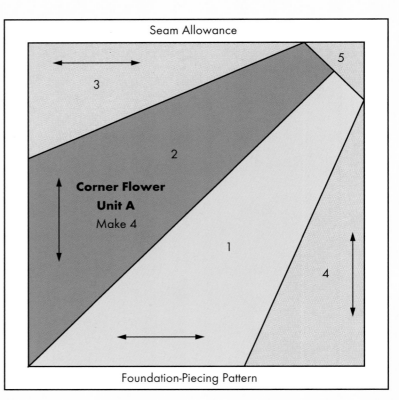

Seam Allowance

3

5

2

**Corner Flower
Unit A**
Make 4

1

4

Foundation-Piecing Pattern

*Patterns are the
reverse of the
finished block.*

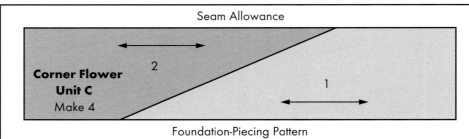

Seam Allowance

2

**Corner Flower
Unit C**
Make 4

1

Foundation-Piecing Pattern

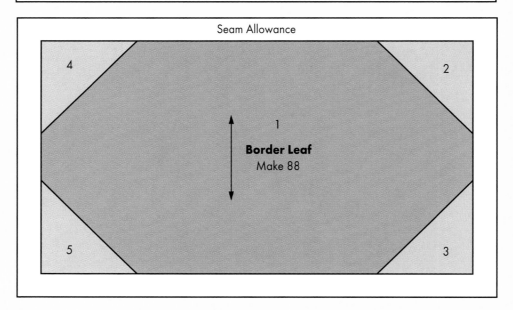

Seam Allowance

4

2

1

Border Leaf
Make 88

5

3

Trip to New York

CHALLENGING ▶ ▶ ▶

By Irene Berry

Faye Anderson's *Across Kansas* quilt pattern inspired Irene Berry of Arvada, Colorado, to make her own version. Using a quarter-circle paper-foundation pieced New York Beauty arc, Irene created *Trip to New York*. Spiky patches in the borders and additional paper-pieced flowers in the border corners complete this eye-catching quilt.

GETTING STARTED

Wash and press fabrics. Cut the patches and other pieces as listed in the materials and cutting box. Refer to page 87 for Quilting Basics.

Designed and made by Irene Berry.

Block Size:		9"
Quilt Size:		44" x 62"
Requirements are based on 42" fabric width.		
Read all instructions before cutting.		
Materials	**Yards**	**Cutting**
Black Solid	1/2	
bias binding		2 1/4" x 6 3/4 yards
Black & Gray Prints	4 1/2	24 A, 96 B, 96 C patches;
		scraps for foundation-pieced block,
		border and corner units; squares
		and rectangles for borders
Bright Prints	2 1/2	96 D patches;
		scraps for foundation-pieced block,
		border, and corner units
Backing	2 7/8	2 panels 34" x 48"
Batting		4" longer and wider than quilt top

MAKING THE BLOCKS

1. Trace or photocopy ninety-six pieced arcs.
2. Foundation piece the fabric units in numerical order.
3. Make ninety-six pieced arcs.
4. Mark the sewing line at the edge of the paper all around. Trim the arcs, leaving 1/4" seam allowances beyond the drawn line.
5. Make templates for A, B, C, and D patches. Each block requires one A patch and four C patches cut from the same fabric, and four B patches cut from another fabric. The designer achieved an interesting look for this quilt by varying the value placement in the Nine-Patch portion of the blocks. In some of the blocks, the A and C patches are lighter than the B patches, and in others, the values are reversed.
6. Sew or appliqué the curved edge of a D patch to each arc, matching dots and seams.
7. Remove the paper.
8. Join one A patch, four B patches, and four C patches to make the block center, referring to the block piecing.

9. Sew four pieced arcs to each pieced center, matching dots.

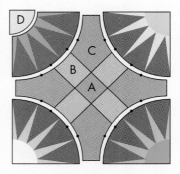

Block Piecing

10. Make twenty-four blocks.

ASSEMBLING THE QUILT TOP

1. Join the blocks in six rows of four blocks each. Join the rows.
2. Trace or photocopy fourteen border units and four each of 1/2 corner unit.
3. Make fourteen border units, sewing the fabric units in numerical order.
4. Make four complete corner units, sewing the fabric units in numerical order.
5. Cut approximately twenty-six 4 1/2" black and gray squares and approximately twenty 1 1/2" x 4 1/2" black and gray rectangles.

6. Referring to the quilt photo, note the random piecing of the borders. To achieve this look, cut some of the border units in half or thirds. Join border units, squares, and rectangles randomly to make two 4½" x 36½" borders and two 4½" x 54½" borders. Cut additional squares and rectangles if needed to reach the required lengths.

7. Sew a long, pieced border to each side.

8. Sew a corner unit to each end of short, pieced borders, placing each corner unit as shown in the quilt photo. Sew borders to the top and bottom.

9. Remove the paper.

QUILTING AND FINISHING

1. Mark the quilting lines on the B, C, and D patches and on the arcs, as indicated on the patterns.

2. Layer the quilt backing, batting, and top.

3. Baste.

4. Quilt as marked.

5. Trim quilt backing and batting even with the quilt top.

6. Make bias binding, referring to bias binding instructions on page 89.

7. Bind the quilt.

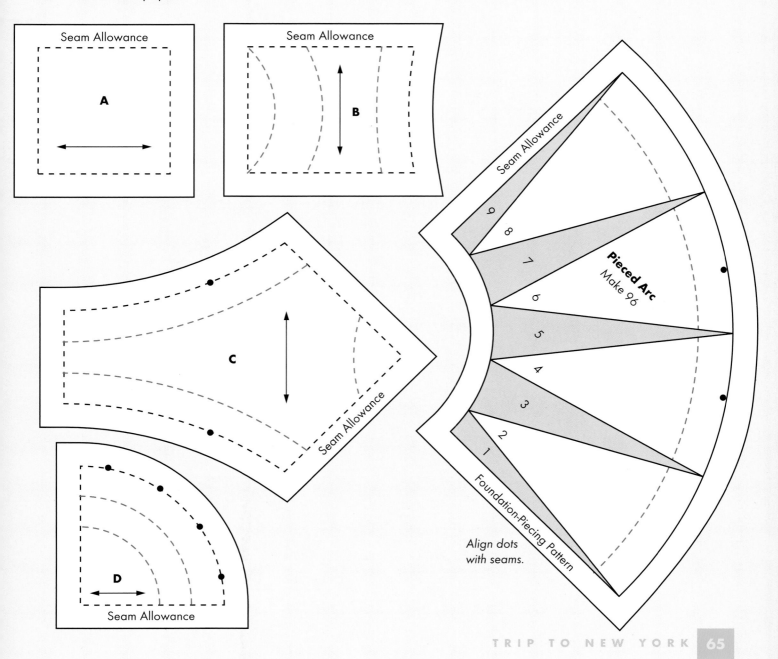

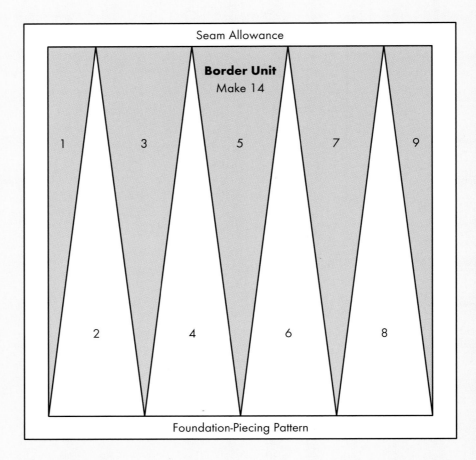

Seam Allowance

Border Unit
Make 14

1 3 5 7 9

2 4 6 8

Foundation-Piecing Pattern

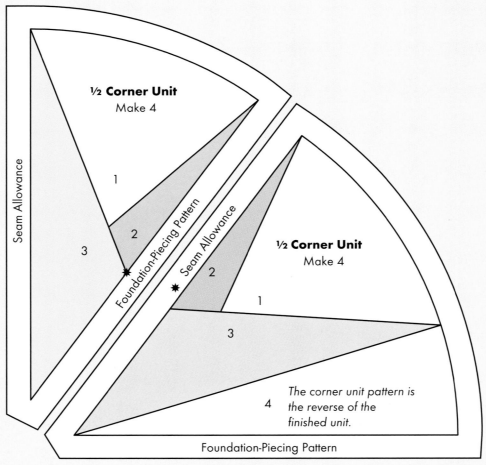

½ **Corner Unit**
Make 4

Seam Allowance

Foundation-Piecing Pattern

1

3

2

Seam Allowance

2

½ **Corner Unit**
Make 4

1

3

4

The corner unit pattern is the reverse of the finished unit.

Foundation-Piecing Pattern

Dandelion

By Keiko Miyamoto

A childhood memory inspired Keiko Miyamoto of Wako-shi, Japan, to design this delightful quilt. As a girl, she played in a large field of dandelions, represented by the thirteen paper-foundation pieced blocks. The "fuzzy" phase of the flower appears in the white circles appliquéd to the borders, and jagged leaves are suggested in the points of the sashing. This challenging pattern requires a thorough knowledge of paper-foundation piecing techniques.

Designed and made by Keiko Miyamoto.

MATERIALS AND CUTTING

Block Size:		9"
Quilt Size:		67½" x 67½"

Requirements are based on 42" fabric width.

Borders include 2″ extra length plus seam allowances.

Read all instructions before cutting.

Materials	Yards	Cutting
White Solid	1/3	15 A, 68 F, 78 G circles
Blue Print	5 1/8	52 B, 8 D, 4 E patches
borders (sides)		2 at 8" x 70"
borders (top/bottom)		2 at 8" x 55"
Yellow/Gold Scraps	1	13 A patches
Aqua/Green Scraps	2 1/4	36 C patches
Prairie Point Scraps	3/4	208 2" squares
Binding	5/8	8 strips 2 1/4" x 42"
Backing	4 1/4	2 panels 36" x 72"
Batting		4" longer and wider than quilt top

 TIP

Fabric Tip

- Cut borders and large patches first from the blue background fabric. Use remaining blue background fabric for paper-foundation piecing.

GETTING STARTED

Wash and press fabrics. Cut the patches and other pieces as listed in the materials and cutting box and as shown in the rotary-cutting illustrations. Refer to page 87 for Quilting Basics.

MAKING THE BLOCKS

1. Trace or photocopy fifty-two petal units.
2. If desired, follow the designer's lead and piece some of the flower petals. To piece petals, sew two strips of yellow/gold fabrics, each 2½" wide. Likewise, sew two strips 1½" and 3½" wide to achieve a different look. Make as many strips as needed for the petal units to be constructed in this manner.

3. Use the pieced fabric for #2, #4, #6, and #8 patches, aligning the seams with the dotted lines on the pattern.
4. Foundation-piece the fabric units in numerical order.
5. Remove the paper.
6. Sew a B patch to each petal unit, matching dots with seams.
7. Join four units to make a block.

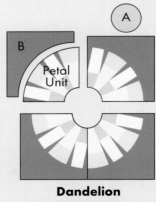

**Dandelion
Block Piecing**
Make 13

8. Appliqué an A patch over the raw edges in the center of the block.
9. Make thirteen blocks.

ASSEMBLING THE QUILT TOP

1. Trace or photocopy seventy-two sash units. Paper-piece these units in numerical order; then sew one to each side of a C strip to make a sash.

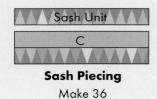

Sash Piecing

Make 36

Edge Unit

Make 12

Setting Square Piecing

Make 12

2. Make thirty-six sashes.

3. Trace or photocopy twelve edge units and twenty-four setting-square units. Sew the fabric units in numerical order. Join two setting-square units to make a square, referring to the setting square piecing.

4. Make twelve setting squares and twelve edge units.

5. Remove the paper.

6. Sew the blocks, sashes, setting squares, edge units, and D and E patches into diagonal rows, referring to the partial quilt assembly. Join the rows. Sew remaining two E patches to opposite corners to complete the center of the quilt top.

7. Sew short blue borders to the top and bottom and long blue borders to the sides.

8. Appliqué white A, F, and G circles randomly on the borders and D and E patches.

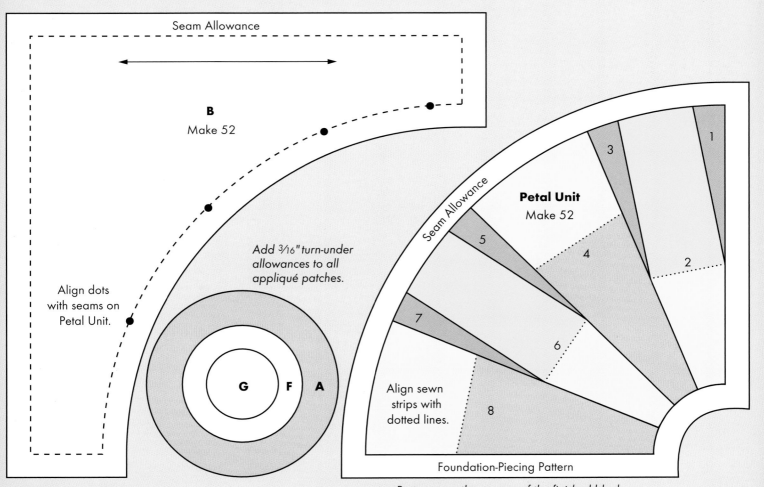

Patterns are the reverse of the finished block.

QUILTING AND FINISHING

1. Layer the quilt backing, batting, and top.

2. Baste.

3. Quilt in-the-ditch around the dandelions and white circles and in the long seams of the sashes, setting squares, and edge units.

4. Mark and quilt a grid in the blue fabric of the background and borders.

5. Make individual prairie points by folding each 2" square in half diagonally, then in half again. Press the folds.

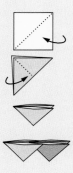

6. Fold the quilt backing out of the way, and with raw edges even with the edges of the quilt top, position fifty-two prairie points on each side. Arrange and pin the points to fill the length of the side evenly. The two points at the corners should just meet. Baste in place and remove pins.

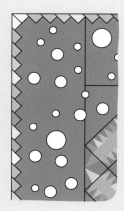

7. Trim quilt backing and batting even with the quilt top.

8. Join 2¼"-wide strips end to end to make the binding.

9. Bind the quilt.

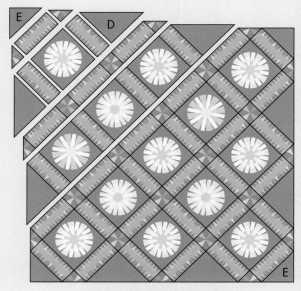

Partial Quilt Assembly

Rotary Cutting
Measurements include ¼" seam allowance. Align arrows with lengthwise or crosswise grain of fabric.

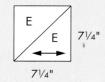

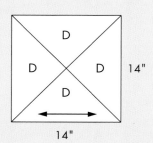

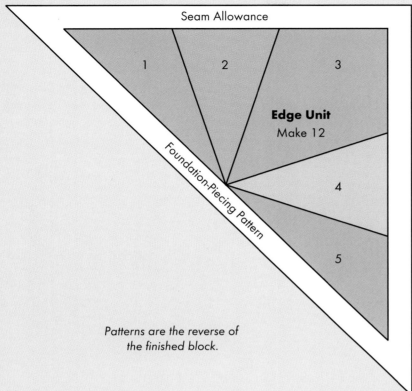

Seam Allowance

1   2   3

Edge Unit
Make 12

Foundation-Piecing Pattern

4

5

Patterns are the reverse of
the finished block.

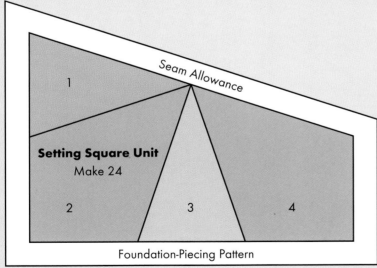

Seam Allowance

1

Setting Square Unit
Make 24

2   3   4

Foundation-Piecing Pattern

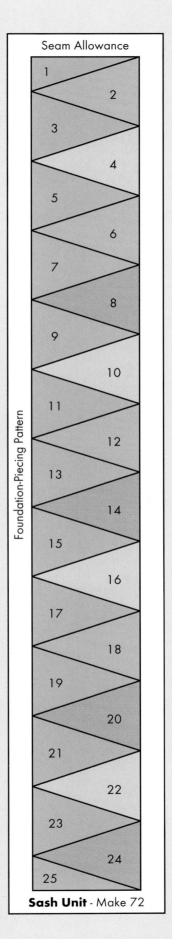

Seam Allowance

1
2
3
4
5
6
7
8
9
10
11
12
13
14
15
16
17
18
19
20
21
22
23
24
25

Foundation-Piecing Pattern

Sash Unit - Make 72

Indian Wedding Ring

by Cynthia Caroff

Cynthia Caroff of Fair Oaks, California, needed to make a quilt for a show, but was suffering from "quilter's block." A photo of *Manitoulin,* a quilt by Elsie Moser, in *American Quilter,* finally inspired her. Although she had planned to use commercial fabric, she ultimately dyed twenty yards for the quilt.

The block is also known as Pickle Dish and Sweetwater Quilt. Cynthia pieced her quilt using templates produced by Quilting From the Heartland. The pattern has been adapted for paper-foundation piecing.

Designed and made by Cynthia Caroff.

MATERIALS AND CUTTING

Block Size: 15"

Quilt Size: 73" x 73"

Requirements are based on 42" fabric width.

Borders include 2" extra length plus seam allowances.

Read all instructions before cutting.

Materials	Yards	Cutting
Gold Scraps	3	25 B, 12 C, 4 D patches
Bright Scraps	3	62 strips 2" x 21"; 64 A patches
Light Scraps	2	66 strips 2" x 21"
Green	3/8	
inner borders (sides)		2 at 1¾" x 62½" (cut crosswise and pieced)
inner borders (top/bottom)		2 at 1¾" x 65" (cut crosswise and pieced)
Gold	2¼*	
outer borders (sides)		2 at 5¾" x 65"
outer borders (top/bottom)		2 at 5¾" x 75½"
Purple	5/8	
binding		8 strips 2¼" x 42"
Backing	4½	2 panels 39" x 77"
Batting		4" longer and wider than quilt top

* Only 1¼ yards are needed if gold borders are cut crosswise and pieced.

Fabric Tip

- The designer used several different fabrics in the borders, joining them in a manner that gives the appearance of continuing the arc of the blocks.

GETTING STARTED

Wash and press fabrics. Cut the patches and other pieces as listed in the materials and cutting box. Refer to page 87 for Quilting Basics.

MAKING THE BLOCKS

1. Trace or photocopy 128 arcs.
2. Foundation-piece the fabric units in numerical order, using bright fabric scraps for the inner triangles of the arc and lighter fabrics for the outer triangles. Some quilters prefer to remove the paper from the arcs before further piecing; others leave the paper on until the quilt top is finished.

3. Mark the dots on A and B patches to help align the seams of the arcs. Make 64 arc units, sewing one arc unit to an A patch and matching the placement dots on the A patch with the patch points of the arc. Use a partial seam, as indicated by the ✶, when sewing the first arc in place. When sewing the curved seams in the units, place the foundation-pieced arcs on top. This will make the intersecting seam lines visible, which will help avoid sewing across any of the points. Press seam allowances toward the A patches.

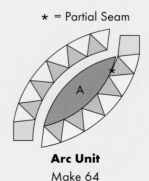

✶ = Partial Seam

Arc Unit
Make 64

4. Join one B patch and four arc units to make one block, aligning the dots with the seams as before.

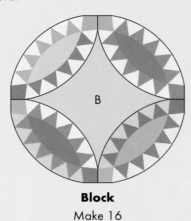

Block
Make 16

5. Make 16 blocks.

ASSEMBLING THE QUILT TOP

1. Join the blocks and additional B patches in four rows of four blocks each, referring to the quilt assembly. Add C and D patches.
2. Remove the paper (if not done earlier).

Quilt Assembly

3. Sew short, narrow green borders to the sides and trim. Sew long, narrow green borders to the top and bottom and trim.
4. Sew short gold borders to the sides and trim. Sew long gold borders to the top and bottom and trim.

QUILTING AND FINISHING

1. Mark the quilting motif in B, C, and D patches.
2. Layer the quilt backing, batting, and top.
3. Baste.
4. Quilt in-the-ditch around the patches.
5. Quilt the motifs as marked. Quilt the outer border using the complete arc unit as a guide for the outer shape of each motif; then echo-quilt inside each arc.
6. Trim quilt backing and batting even with the quilt top.
7. Join 2¼"-wide strips end to end to make the binding.
8. Bind the quilt.

¼ **B**
Make 16

½ **C**
Make 12

D
Make 4

Place on fold for B.

Add ¼" seam allowance for C & D.

Place on fold for B & C.

Add ¼" seam allowance for D.

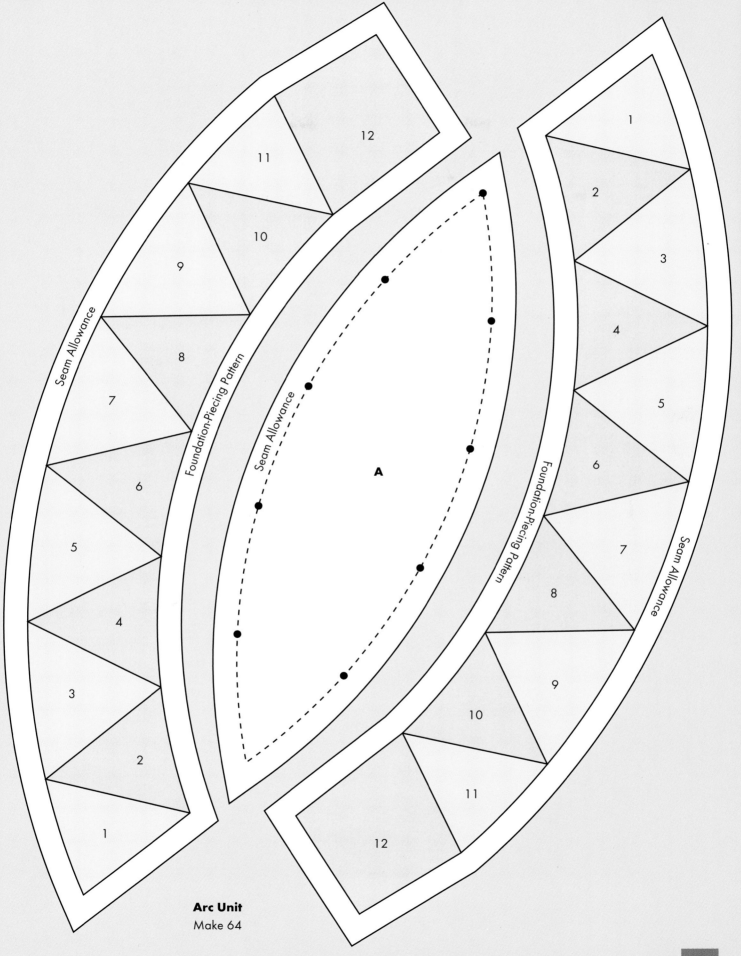

Seam Allowance

Foundation-Piecing Pattern

Seam Allowance

A

Foundation-Piecing Pattern

Seam Allowance

Arc Unit
Make 64

Apache Trail

Mystery surrounds *Apache Trail*. The present owner, Madelyn Gibbs of Arvada, Colorado, purchased this beauty at an antique store near Rocky Mountain National Park. The only information known about the quilt is that it originally came from Tennessee.

The setting of the block units makes this block unique. The corner units are rotated so the fans are facing inward—unlike similar settings.

MATERIALS AND CUTTING

Block Size: 14" [14"]

Quilt Sizes: Wide Twin (shown), [Queen Coverlet] 74" x 88" [92" x 106"]

Requirements are based on 42" fabric width.

Borders include 2" extra length plus seam allowances.

Read all instructions before cutting.

Materials	Yards	Cutting	Materials	Yards	Cutting
Wide Twin			**Queen Coverlet**		
White Solid	5¼		**White Solid**	7⅝	
outer borders (side)		2 at 5" x 81½"	outer borders (sides)		2 at 6" x 97½"
outer borders (top/bottom)		2 at 5" x 76½"	outer borders (top/bottom)		2 at 6" x 94½"
		320 C patches			480 C patches
Yellow Solid	3¼		**Yellow Solid**	4¼	
inner borders (sides)		2 at 5" x 72½"	inner borders (sides)		2 at 6" x 86½"
inner borders (top/bottom)		2 at 5" x 67½"	inner borders (top/bottom)		2 at 6" x 83½"
binding		5 strips 2¼" x 70"	binding		5 strips 2¼" x 84"
		320 B patches			480 B patches
Assorted Scraps	4½	Arc units	**Assorted Scraps**	6⅝	Arc units
Backing	5⅜	2 panels 40" x 92"	**Backing**	8½	3 panels 37" x 96"
Batting		4" longer and wider than quilt top	**Batting**		4" longer and wider than quilt top

Directions are for both the wide twin comforter and the queen coverlet. Information that differs for the queen size is given in [ ].

GETTING STARTED

Wash and press fabrics. Cut the patches and other pieces as listed in the materials and cutting box. Refer to page 87 for Quilting Basics.

MAKING THE BLOCKS

1. Trace or photocopy 320 [480] arcs-units.
2. Sew the fabric units in numerical order.
3. Remove the paper.
4. Join the arc with a B patch and a C patch to make one block unit.
5. Make sixteen block units.
6. Join sixteen block units to make one block, referring to block piecing for placement.
7. Make 20 [30] blocks.

ASSEMBLING THE QUILT TOP

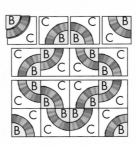

Block Piecing
Make 20 [30]

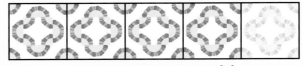

Row Assembly Make 5 [6]

Wide twin comforter is shown in darker colors. Queen size includes the complete diagram.

Piecing Tips

- Each block is composed of sixteen identical block units, arranged in a setting that creates this pattern. The arc of each block unit can be pieced with twelve A patches, or can be foundation pieced.

- Refer to "The Right Curves" for information on working with curved patches.

1. Join 4 [5] blocks to make a row.
2. Make 5 [6] rows. Press the seam allowances of every other row in the same direction.
3. Join the rows, setting rows four by five [five by six].
4. Sew the inner borders to the sides of the quilt and trim. Sew the inner borders to the top and bottom. Press the seam allowances toward the borders.
5. Sew the outer borders to the sides of the quilt and trim. Sew the outer borders to the top and bottom. Press the seam allowances toward the borders.

QUILTING AND FINISHING

1. Mark the cable-quilting motif in the inner and outer borders, beginning at the center of each border and working outward toward the corners as shown in quilting placement. Rotate the half pattern to complete the motif. Note the different center starting points for each border on the quilting motif.

2. Layer the quilt backing, batting, and top.
3. Baste.
4. Outline quilt the B and C patches and the quilt borders as marked, referring to quilting placement.
5. Trim quilt backing and batting even with the quilt top.
6. Join 2¼"-wide strips end to end to make the binding.
7. Bind the quilt.

THE RIGHT CURVES

Apache Trail has three sections, each with at least one curved seam. The following hints may be helpful when cutting and sewing these patches together.

When cutting curved patches, use a small-blade rotary cutter to accurately negotiate the curves. Gluing a few dots cut from sandpaper to the back of the template will help keep it in place while cutting. Cutting mats may have ruts and bumps from straight-line cutting, which can affect how accurately the curves are cut. To assure accuracy, flip the mat over to avoid these ruts and bumps.

Pin the B patch to the inside, or concave, curve of the A-patch unit at the ends, the middle, and a few places in between. Clipping the seam allowances is not necessary. If sewing by machine, sew the patches together with the B patch on the bottom, stopping frequently with the needle down to adjust the fabric to lay flat under the needle and presser foot. Then pin the C patch on top of the A-B unit and sew in place.

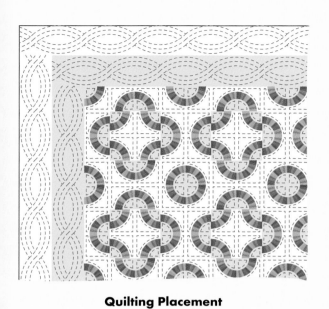

Quilting Placement

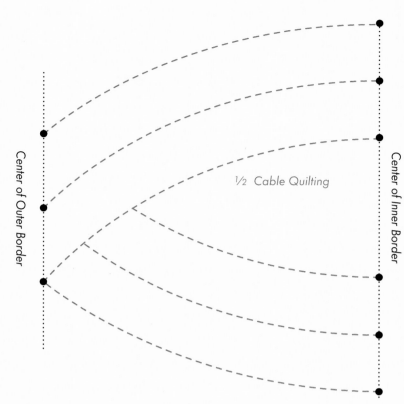

Center of Outer Border

Center of Inner Border

½ Cable Quilting

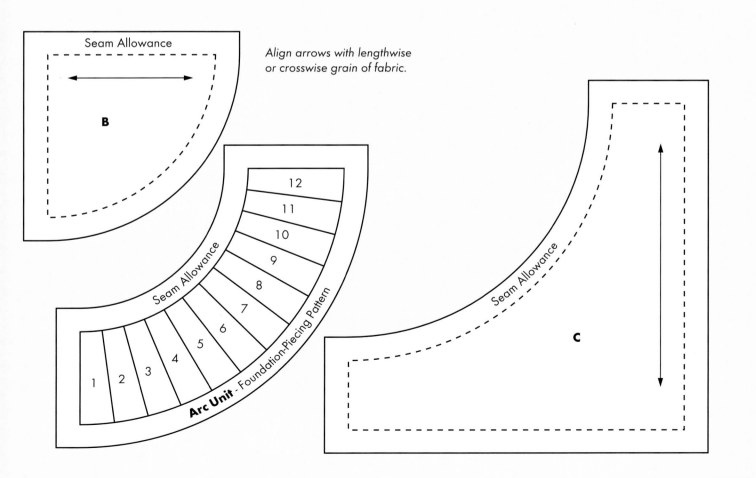

Seam Allowance

B

Align arrows with lengthwise or crosswise grain of fabric.

Seam Allowance

12
11
10
9
8
7
6
5
4
3
2
1

Arc Unit - Foundation-Piecing Pattern

Seam Allowance

C

Thanksgiving Wedding Ring

CHALLENGING ▶ ▶ ▶

By Irene Berry

Fabrics in colors inspired by fall skies and turning leaves were used to make an anniversary quilt for the designer's parents, who were married on Thanksgiving. The border appliqué was designed using elements from antique quilts: for love, the pomegranate (or love apple), and for hospitality, the pineapple.

By the time this scrap quilt was nearing completion, its maker realized she wasn't ready to part with it, so she made a different quilt for her parents' anniversary.

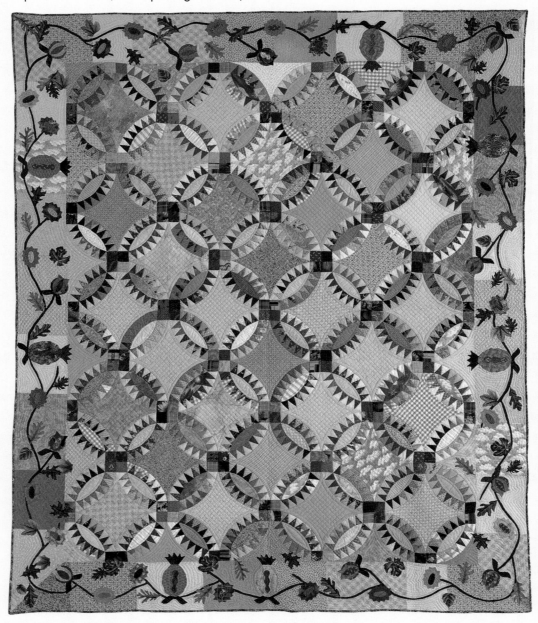

Designed and made by Irene Berry.

MATERIALS AND CUTTING

Block Size:	15½"	[15½"]
Quilt Sizes: Double Comforter (shown), [Sofa Quilt]	77" x 92½"	[56½" x 72"]

Requirements are based on 42" fabric width.

Borders include 2" extra length plus seam allowances.

Read all instructions before cutting.

Materials	Yards	Cutting	Materials	Yards	Cutting
Double Comforter			**Sofa Quilt**		
Light Prints*	scraps		**Light Prints***	scraps	
foundation-piecing		#1, 3, 5, 7, 9, 11, 13 triangles; 80 A, 32 C, 14 D, 4 E, 31 F** patches	foundation-piecing		1, 3, 5, 7, 9, 11, 13 triangles; 48 A, 8 C, 10 D, 4 E patches
Medium/Dark Prints	scraps		**Medium/Dark Prints**	scraps	
foundation-piecing		#2, 4, 6, 8, 10, 12; 160 B patches	foundation-piecing		2, 4, 6, 8, 10, 12 triangles; 96 B patches
appliqué		G, H, I, Ir, J, K, L, M, N, O, P shapes	appliqué		none for this size
Green Prints	scraps		**Green Prints**		none for this size
bias strips		4 at 1¼" x 30"			
bias strips		18 at 1¼" x 23"			
Medium Blue Print		none for this size	**Medium Blue Print**	2¼	
			borders (sides)		2 at 5½" x 74½"
			borders (top/bottom)		2 at 5½" x 59"
Gold Print	¾		**Gold Print**	⅝	
binding		10 strips 2¼" x 38"	binding		8 strips 2¼" x 37"
Backing	7¼	3 panels 33" x 81"	**Backing**	3⅝	2 panels 39" x 61"
Batting		4" longer and wider than quilt top	**Batting**		4" longer and wider than quilt top

* If using one fabric for the A, C, D and E patches, 9⅛ [5⅝] yards will be needed. Less yardage will be needed if grain lines are disregarded.

** To make the pieced border, join thirty-one F patches end to end to make one strip. Cut this strip into two 8" x 95" lengths for the sides and two 8" x 79½" strips for the top and bottom. If making a one-fabric border, 2⅞ yards will be needed to cut the strips as given.

Directions are for both the sofa quilt, which has no appliqué, and the double comforter. Information that differs for the sofa size is given in [ ].

Fabric Tips

- Yardage amounts are given for the backings, bindings, and sofa border only. The double comforter border is first pieced with scrap F patches and then cut to border lengths; the sofa quilt has a single-fabric border. To replicate this quilt, use scraps for all the piecing and appliqué.

- The designer's fabric choices for the background and borders (A patches, C–F patches, and odd-numbered foundation patches) are light blue, pink, and gray prints. The medium to dark fabrics used in the foundation-pieced units and appliqué are warm-colored prints in reds, golds, and browns, with a few greens tossed into the mix. The bias stems are made using a variety of green prints.

- The designer added appliqué randomly around the border. For this reason, the number of patches required is not listed.

- The designer chose fabrics with motifs in all scales, which adds eye-catching interest.

GETTING STARTED

Wash and press fabrics. Cut the patches and other pieces as listed in the materials and cutting box. Refer to page 87 for Quilting Basics.

MAKING THE BLOCKS

1. Trace or photocopy 160 [96] arcs.
2. Foundation piece the fabric units in numerical order, using bright fabric scraps for the inner triangles of the arc and lighter fabrics for the outer triangles. Some quilters prefer to remove the paper from the arcs before further piecing; others leave the paper on until the quilt top is finished.
3. Mark the dots on A and C patches to help align the seams of the arcs. Make 80 [48] arc units, sewing one arc unit to A patch and matching the placement dots on the A patch with the patch points of the arc. Sew B patches to a second arc unit and sew to the opposite side of the A patch. When sewing the curved seams in the units, place the foundation-pieced arcs on top. This will make the intersecting

seam lines visible, which will help avoid sewing across any of the points. Press seam allowances toward the A patches.

Unit Piecing
Make 80 [48]

4. Join one C patch and four arc units to make one block, aligning the dots with the seams as before.

Block
Make 20 [12]

5. Make 20 [12] blocks.

ASSEMBLING THE QUILT TOP

1. Join the blocks and additional C patches in five rows of four blocks each, referring to the quilt assembly on page 84. Add D and E patches.
2. Remove the paper (if not done earlier).
3. For the pieced border, join the F patches to make one long strip. Cut this strip into two 95" lengths for the sides and two 79½" strips for the top and bottom. [Cut the medium blue print borders as given in the yardage box.]
4. Matching centers, sew the borders to the quilt and miter the corners.
5. Trim the seam allowances to ¼" and press open.
6. If making the sofa quilt, skip to Quilting and Finishing.

APPLIQUÉING THE BORDER

1. Make the bias stems.
2. Appliqué the bias stems on the border, referring to appliqué and quilting placement. This diagram shows an approximate placement of the stems, appliqué, and quilting lines.
3. Reverse-appliqué the N and O patches as follows. First, mark the outline of the N patch on the O patch. Center the N patch under the O patch, right side up, and baste ¼" out from the marked line. Prepare the outside edges of the O patch for appliqué and then blindstitch the N/O patch in place on the border. Trim away the O-patch fabric ³⁄₁₆" inside the marked line and clip the curves as needed. Turn under the raw edges along the line and blindstitch the fold through all layers. Remove the basting.

4. Prepare the G–P patches for appliqué using your favorite method. In alphabetical order within each motif, blindstitch the patches to the border.

QUILTING AND FINISHING

1. Layer the quilt backing, batting, and top.
2. Baste.
3. Quilt in-the-ditch around the arcs and B patches.
4. Outline-quilt ½" inside the A and C patch seams; then quilt a grid in the C patches, spacing the lines ½" apart.
5. Echo-quilt the D and E patches and the appliqué, spacing the lines approximately ½" apart.
6. Quilt inside the appliqué patches as shown. [Quilt the arc patches and border in-the-ditch. Echo-quilt the D and E patches and grid quilt the C patches as shown. Then quilt parallel lines 1" apart in the border.]

Appliqué and Quilting Placement

7. Trim quilt backing and batting even with the quilt top.
8. Join 2¼"-wide strips end to end to make the binding.
9. Bind the quilt.

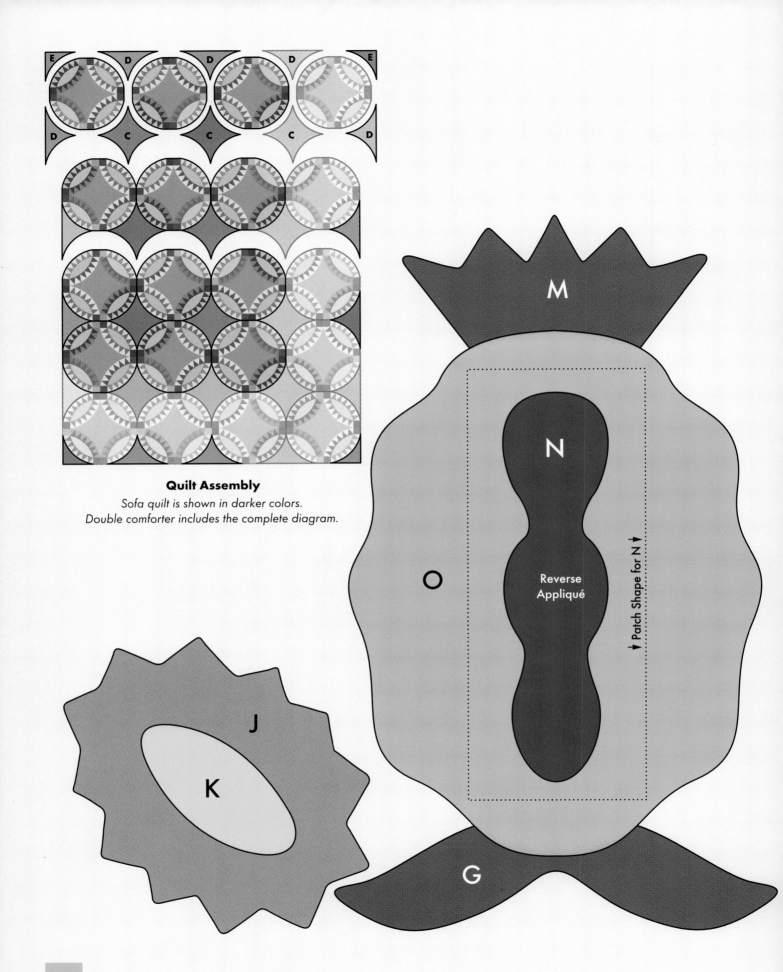

Quilt Assembly

Sofa quilt is shown in darker colors.
Double comforter includes the complete diagram.

M

N

O

Reverse
Appliqué

↓ Patch Shape for N ↓

J

K

G

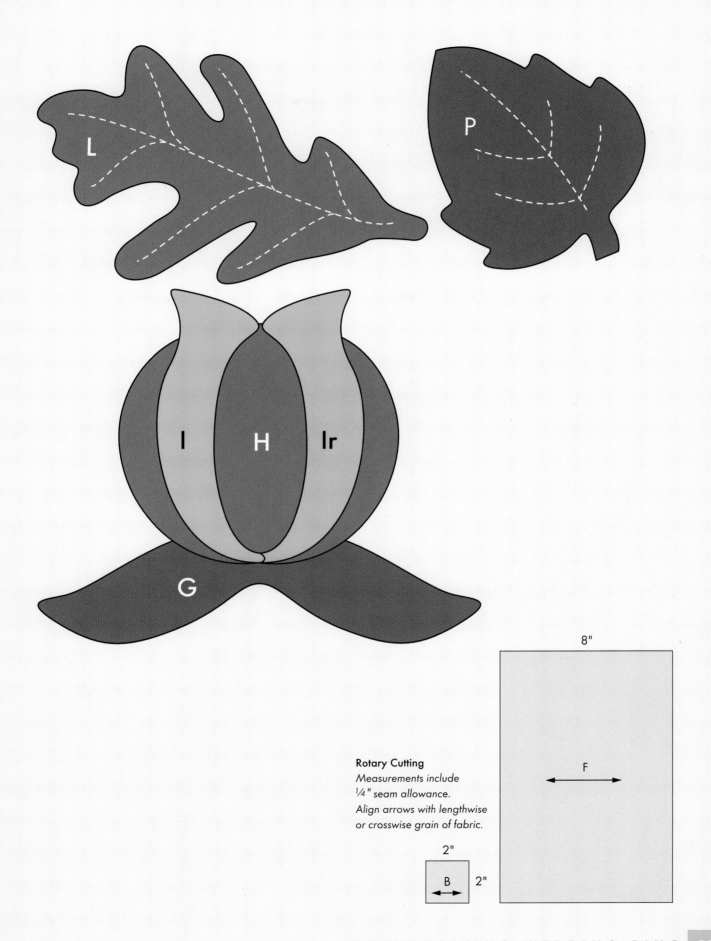

Rotary Cutting
Measurements include
¼" seam allowance.
Align arrows with lengthwise
or crosswise grain of fabric.

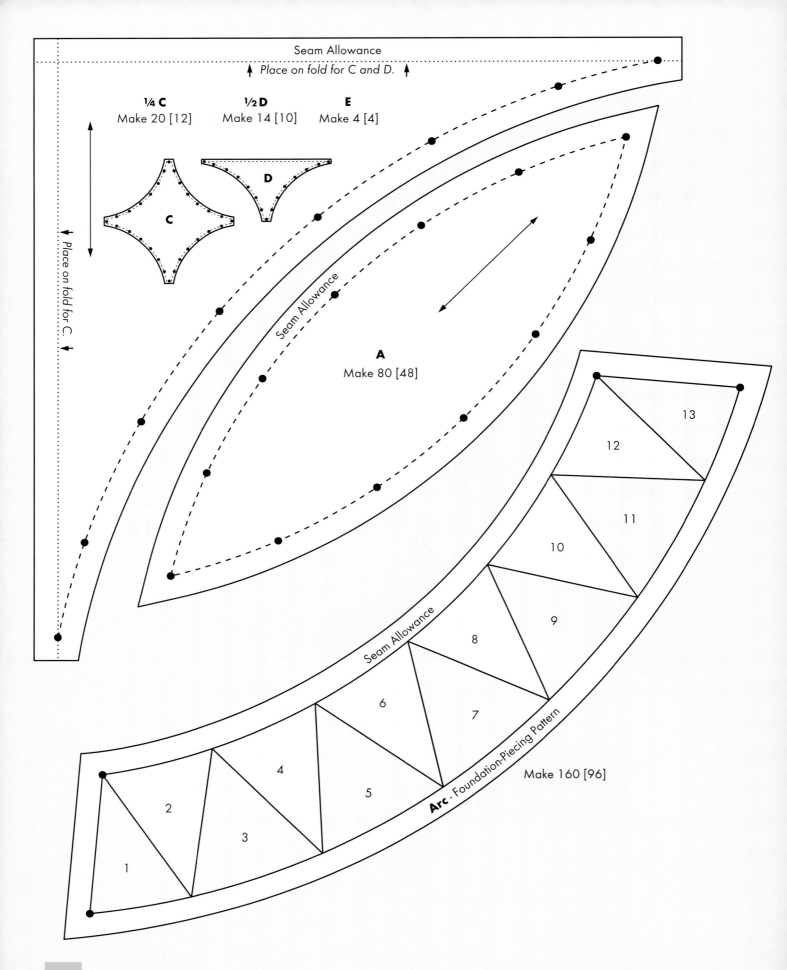

Seam Allowance

Place on fold for C and D.

¼ C
Make 20 [12]

½ D
Make 14 [10]

E
Make 4 [4]

D

C

Place on fold for C.

Seam Allowance

A
Make 80 [48]

Seam Allowance

13

12

11

10

9

8

7

6

5

4

3

2

1

Arc - Foundation-Piecing Pattern

Make 160 [96]

Quilting Basics

Fabric requirements are based on a 42"-width; many fabrics shrink when washed, and widths vary by manufacturer. In cutting instructions, strips are generally cut on the crosswise grain.

GENERAL GUIDELINES

Seam Allowances

A ¼" seam allowance is used for most projects. It's a good idea to do a test seam before you begin sewing to check that your ¼" is accurate.

Pressing

In general, press seams toward the darker fabric. Press lightly in an up-and-down motion. Avoid using a very hot iron or over-ironing, which can distort shapes and blocks.

Borders

When border strips are to be cut on the crosswise grain, diagonally piece the strips together to achieve the needed lengths.

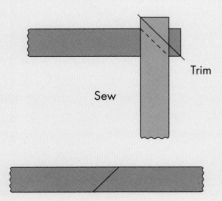

Sew

Trim

Butted Borders

In most cases the side borders are sewn on first. When you have finished the quilt top, measure it through the center vertically. This will be the length to cut the side borders. Place pins at the centers of all four sides of the quilt top, as well as in the center of each side border strip. Pin the side borders to the quilt top first, matching the center pins. Using a ¼" seam allowance, sew the borders to the quilt top and press.

Measure horizontally across the center of the quilt top including the side borders. This will be the length to cut the top and bottom borders. Repeat pinning, sewing, and pressing.

Mitered Corner Borders

Measure the length of the quilt top and add two times the width of your border, plus 5". This is the length you need to cut or piece the side for borders.

Place pins at centers of all four sides of the quilt top and both side borders. Pin, matching center pins, and stitch the strips to the sides of the quilt top. Stop and backstitch at the seam allowance line, ¼" in from the edge. The excess length will extend beyond each edge. Press seams toward border.

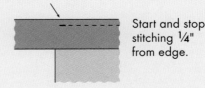

Start and stop stitching ¼" from edge.

To determine the length needed for the top and bottom border the same way, measure the width of the quilt top through the center, including each side border. Add 5" to this measurement. Cut or piece these border strips. Again, pin, stitch up to the 1/4" seam line, and backstitch. The border strips extend beyond each end.

To create the miter, lay the corner on the ironing board. Working with the quilt right side up, lay one strip on top of the adjacent border.

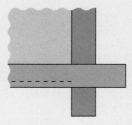

Fold the top border strip under itself so that it meets the edge of the outer border and forms a 45° angle. Press and pin the fold in place.

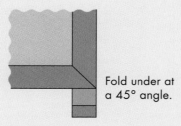

Fold under at a 45° angle.

Position a 90° angle triangle or ruler over the corner to check that the corner is flat and square. When everything is in place press the fold firmly.

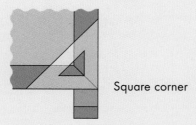

Square corner

Fold the center section of the top diagonally from the corner, right sides together, and align the long edges of the border strips. On the wrong side, place pins near the pressed fold in the corner to secure the border strips.

Beginning at the inside corner, backstitch and stitch along the fold toward the outside point, being careful not to allow any stretching to occur.

Backstitch at the end. Trim the excess border fabric to 1/4" seam allowance. Press the seam open.

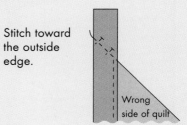

Stitch toward the outside edge.

Wrong side of quilt

Batting

The type of batting to use is a personal decision; consult your local quilt shop. Cut batting approximately 2" larger on all sides than your quilt top.

Layering

Spread the backing wrong side up and tape the edges down with masking tape. (If you are working on carpet you can use T-pins to secure the backing to the carpet.) Center the batting on top, smoothing out any folds. Place the quilt top right side up on top of the batting and backing, making sure it is centered.

Basting

If planning to machine quilt, pin-baste the quilt layers together with safety pins placed a minimum of 3"–4" apart. Begin basting in the center and move toward the edges first in vertical, then horizontal, rows.

If planning to hand-quilt, baste the layers together with thread using a long needle and light-colored thread. Knot one end of the thread. Using stitches approximately the length of the needle, begin in the center and move out toward the edges.

Quilting

Quilting, whether by hand or machine, enhances the pieced or appliqué design of the quilt. Many quilting options are possible, including quilting in-the-ditch, echoing the pieced or appliqué motifs, using patterns from quilting design books and stencils, or free-motion quilting. Suggested quilting patterns are included for some of the projects.

Binding

Double-Fold Straight-Grain Binding

Trim excess batting and backing from the quilt. For a ¼" finished binding, cut the strips 2¼" wide and piece together with a diagonal seam to make a continuous binding strip.

Press the seams open, then press the entire strip in half lengthwise with wrong sides together. With raw edges even, pin the binding to the edge of the quilt a few inches away from the corner, and leave the first few inches of the binding unattached. Start sewing, using a ¼" seam allowance.

Stop ¼" away from the first corner (see Step 1), backstitch one stitch. Lift the presser foot and rotate the quilt. Fold the binding at a right angle so it extends straight above the quilt (see Step 2). Then bring the binding strip down even with the edge of the quilt (see Step 3). Begin sewing at the folded edge.

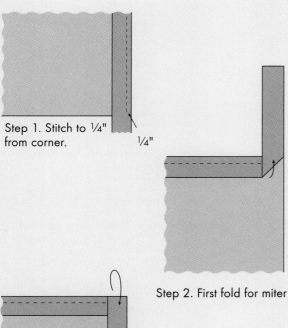

Step 1. Stitch to ¼" from corner.

¼"

Step 2. First fold for miter

Step 3. Second fold alignment. Repeat in the same manner at all corners.

Continuous Bias Binding

A continuous bias involves using the same square sliced in half diagonally but sewing the triangles together so that you continuously cut the marked strips. The same instructions can be used to cut bias for piping. Cut the fabric for the bias binding or piping so it is a square. If yardage is ½ yard, cut an 18" square. Cut the square in half diagonally, creating two triangles.

Sew these triangles together as shown, using a ¼" seam allowance. Press the seam open.

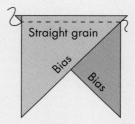

Straight grain

Bias

Bias

Using a ruler, mark the parallelogram with lines spaced the width you need to cut your bias. Cut along the first line about 5".

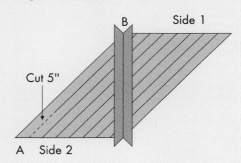

B

Side 1

Cut 5"

A   Side 2

Join Side 1 and Side 2 to form a tube. Line A will line up with the raw edge at B. This will allow the first line to be offset by one stripwidth. Pin the raw ends together, making sure that the lines match. Sew with a ¼" seam allowance. Press seams open.

MACHINE-APPLIQUÉ USING FUSIBLE ADHESIVE

Lay the fusible web sheet paper-side up on the pattern and trace with a pencil. Trace detail lines with a permanent marker for ease in transferring to the fabric.

Use paper-cutting scissors to roughly cut out the pieces. Leave at least a 1/4" border.

Following manufacturer's instructions, fuse the web patterns to the wrong side of the appliqué fabric. It helps to use an appliqué-pressing sheet to avoid getting the adhesive on your iron or ironing board.

Cut out the pieces along the pencil line. Do not remove the paper yet.

Transfer the detail lines to the fabric by placing the piece on a light table or up to the window and marking the fabric. Use pencil for this task—the lines will be covered by thread.

Remove the paper and position the appliqué piece on project. Be sure the web (rough) side is down. Press in place, following the manufacturer's instructions.

Index

Projects:

Apache Trail 76
Colorful Kites 17
Dandelion 67
Fireworks 43
Garden Patch 26
Indian Wedding Ring 72
Party Whirl 22
Pineapple Slices 47
Pink Dogwood 57
Puzzled 13
Rick Rackosaurus 8
Secret Garden 32
Sunflowers 52
Thanksgiving Wedding Ring 80
Trip to New York 63
Wee Houses 39

Useful Information:

Changing Fabric Color to Alter Block Appearance 50
Embroidery-Stitch Illustrations 31,34
Fabric Tips for Working with Freezer Paper 59
Fabric Tip for Working with Silk 44
Paper-Foundation Piecing 101 6
Prairie Points 70
Quilting Basics 87
    Basting 88
    Batting 88
    Binding 89
    Borders 87
    Layering 88
    Machine Appliqué Using Fusible Adhesive 90
    Pressing 87
    Quilting 88
    Seam Allowances 87
Reverse Appliqué 83
The Right Curves (Working With Curved Patches) 78

Notes

Notes

Notes

OTHER FINE BOOKS FROM C&T PUBLISHING

250 Continuous-Line Quilting Designs for Hand, Machine & Long-Arm Quilters, Laura Lee Fritz

Along the Garden Path: More Quilters and Their Gardens, Jean Wells & Valori Wells

An Amish Adventure, 2nd Edition: A Workbook for Color in Quilts, Roberta Horton

Anatomy of a Doll: The Fabric Sculptor's Handbook, Susanna Oroyan

Appliqué 12 Easy Ways!: Charming Quilts, Giftable Projects, & Timeless Techniques, Elly Sienkiewicz

Art of Classic Quiltmaking, The (sc), Harriet Hargrave & Sharyn Craig

Art of Machine Piecing, The: How to Achieve Quality Workmanship Through a Colorful Journey, Sally Collins

Art of Silk Ribbon Embroidery, The, Judith Baker Montano

Artful Ribbon, The: Beauties in Bloom, Candace Kling

At Home with Patrick Lose: Colorful Quilted Projects, Patrick Lose

Baltimore Beauties and Beyond Vol. I (sc): Studies In Classic Album Quilt Appliqué, Elly Sienkiewicz

Best of Baltimore Beauties, The: 95 Patterns for Album Blocks and Borders, Elly Sienkiewicz

Block Magic: Over 50 Fun & Easy Blocks from Squares and Rectangles, Nancy Johnson-Srebro

Bouquet of Quilts, A: Garden-Inspired Projects for the Home, Jennifer Rounds & Cyndy Lyle Rymer

Butterflies & Blooms: Designs for Appliqué & Quilting, Carol Armstrong

Civil War Women: Their Quilts, Their Roles & Activities for Re-Enactors, Barbara Brackman

Color from the Heart: Seven Great Ways to Make Quilts with Colors You Love, Gai Perry

Color Play: Easy Steps to Imaginative Color in Quilts, Joen Wolfrom

Come Listen to my Quilts: •Playful Projects •Mix & Match Designs, Kristina Becker

Cotton Candy Quilts: Using Feed Sacks, Vintage, and Reproduction Fabrics, Mary Mashuta

Crazy Quilt Handbook, The: Revised, 2nd Edition, Judith Baker Montano

Crazy with Cotton: Piecing Together Memories & Themes, Diana Leone

Create Your Own Quilt Labels!, Kim Churbuck

Curves in Motion: Quilt Designs & Techniques, Judy Dales

Cut-Loose Quilts: Stack, Slice, Switch, and Sew, Jan Mullen

Designing the Doll: From Concept to Construction, Susanna Oroyan

Diane Phalen Quilts: 10 Projects to Celebrate The Seasons, Diane Phalen

Do-It-Yourself Framed Quilts: Fast, Fun & Easy Projects, Gai Perry

Easy Pieces: Creative Color Play with two Simple Blocks, Margaret Miller

Elegant Stitches: An Illustrated Stitch Guide & Source Book of Inspiration, Judith Baker Montano

Enchanted Views: Quilts Inspired by Wrought-Iron Designs, Dilys Fronks

Endless Possibilities: Using No-Fail Methods, Nancy Johnson-Srebro

Everything Flowers: Quilts from the Garden, Jean Wells & Valori Wells

Exploring Machine Trapunto: New Dimensions, Hari Walner

Fabric Shopping with Alex Anderson, Alex Anderson

Fabric Stamping Handbook, The: •Fun Projects •Tips & Tricks •Unlimited Possibilities, Jean Ray Laury

Fancy Appliqué: 12 Lessons to Enhance Your Skills, Elly Sienkiewicz

Fantastic Fabric Folding: Innovative Quilting Projects, Rebecca Wat

Fantastic Figures: Ideas and Techniques Using the New Clays, Susanna Oroyan

Finishing the Figure: •Doll Costuming •Embellishments •Accessories, Susanna Oroyan

Floral Stitches: An Illustrated Guide to Floral Stitchery, Judith Baker Montano

Flower Pounding: Quilt Projects for All Ages, Ann Frischkorn & Amy Sandrin

Freddy's House: Brilliant Color in Quilts, Freddy Moran

Free Stuff for Collectors on the Internet, Judy Heim & Gloria Hansen

Free Stuff for Crafty Kids on the Internet, Judy Heim & Gloria Hansen

Free Stuff for Doll Lovers on the Internet, Judy Heim & Gloria Hansen

Free Stuff for Gardeners on the Internet, Judy Heim & Gloria Hansen

Free Stuff for Home Décor on the Internet, Judy Heim & Gloria Hansen

Free Stuff for Home Repair on the Internet, Judy Heim & Gloria Hansen

Free Stuff for Pet Lovers on the Internet, Gloria Hansen

Free Stuff for Quilters on the Internet, 3rd Edition, Judy Heim & Gloria Hansen

Free Stuff for Sewing Fanatics on the Internet, Judy Heim & Gloria Hansen

Free Stuff for Stitchers on the Internet, Judy Heim & Gloria Hansen

Free Stuff for Traveling Quilters on the Internet, Gloria Hansen

Free-Style Quilts: A "No Rules" Approach, Susan Carlson

From Fiber to Fabric: The Essential Guide to Quiltmaking Textiles, Harriet Hargrave

Garden-Inspired Quilts: Design Journals for 12 Quilt Projects, Jean Wells & Valori Wells

Ghost Layers and Color Washes: Three Steps to Spectacular Quilts, Katie Pasquini Masopust

Great Lakes, Great Quilts: 12 Projects Celebrating Quilting Traditions, Marsha MacDowell

Hand Appliqué with Alex Anderson: Seven Projects for Hand Appliqué, Alex Anderson

Hand Quilting with Alex Anderson: Six Projects for First-Time Hand Quilters, Alex Anderson

Heirloom Machine Quilting, Third Edition: Comprehensive Guide to Hand-Quilting Effects Using Your Sewing Machine, Harriet Hargrave

Imagery on Fabric, Second Edition: A Complete Surface Design Handbook, Jean Ray Laury

Impressionist Palette: Quilt Color & Design, Gai Perry

Impressionist Quilts, Gai Perry

In the Nursery: Creative Quilts and Designer Touches, Jennifer Sampou & Carolyn Schmitz

Jacobean Rhapsodies: Composing with 28 Appliqué Designs, Pat Campbell & Mimi Ayers

Judith Baker Montano: Art & Inspirations (sc): Art & Inspirations, Judith Baker Montano

Kaleidoscope Artistry, Cozy Baker

Kaleidoscopes: Wonders of Wonder, Cozy Baker

Kaleidoscopes & Quilts, Paula Nadelstern

Kids Start Quilting with Alex Anderson: •7 Fun & Easy Projects •Quilts for Kids by Kids •Tips for Quilting with Children, Alex Anderson

Laurel Burch Quilts: Kindred Creatures, Laurel Burch

Lone Star Quilts and Beyond: Step-by-Step Projects and Inspiration, Jan Krentz

Machine Embroidery and More: Ten Step-by-Step Projects Using Border Fabrics & Beads, Kristen Dibbs

Make Any Block Any Size: Easy Drawing Method, Unlimited Pattern Possibilities, Sensational Quilt Designs, Joen Wolfrom

Mariner's Compass Quilts: New Directions, Judy Mathieson

Mastering Machine Appliqué, 2nd Edition: The Complete Guide Including: • Invisible Machine Appliqué • Satin Stitch • Blanket Stitch & Much More, Harriet Hargrave

Mastering Quilt Marking: Marking Tools and Techniques, Choosing Stencils, Matching Borders and Corners, Pepper Cory

Measure the Possibilities with Omnigrid®, Nancy Johnson-Srebro

Michael James: Art & Inspirations: Art & Inspirations, Michael James

New England Quilt Museum Quilts, The: Featuring the Story of the Mill Girls. With Instructions for 5 Heirloom Quilts, Jennifer Gilbert

New Sampler Quilt, The, Diana Leone

On the Surface: Thread Embellishment & Fabric Manipulation, Wendy Hill

Paper Piecing Picnic: Fun-Filled Projects for Every Quilter, QNM

Paper Piecing with Alex Anderson: •Tips •Techniques • 6 Projects, Alex Anderson

Patchwork Persuasion: Fascinating Quilts from Traditional Designs, Joen Wolfrom

Photo Transfer Handbook, The: Snap It, Print It, Stitch It!, Jean Ray Laury

Pieced Clothing Variations, Yvonne Porcella

Pieced Flowers, Ruth B. McDowell

Pieced Roman Shades, Terrell Sundermann

Pieced Vegetables, Ruth B. McDowell

Piecing: Expanding the Basics, Ruth B. McDowell

Provence Quilts and Cuisine, Marie-Christine Flocard & Cosabeth Parriaud

Quick Quilts for the Holidays: 11 Projects to Stamp, Stencil, and Sew, Trice Boerens

Quilt It for Kids: 11 Projects, Sports, Animal, Fantasy Themes, For Children of All Ages, Pam Bono

Quilted Garden, The: Design & Make Nature-Inspired Quilts, Jane Sassaman

Quilting Back to Front: Fun & Easy No-Mark Techniques, Larraine Scouler

Quilting with Carol Armstrong: • 30 Quilting Patterns • Appliqué Designs • 16 Projects, Carol Armstrong

Quilting with the Muppets: 15 Fun and Creative Projects, The Jim Henson Company in association with the Sesame Workshop

Quilts for Guys: 15 Fun Projects For Your Favorite Fella, Compilation

Quilts from Europe, Gül Laporte

Quilts from the Civil War: Nine Projects, Historic Notes, Diary Entries, Barbara Brackman

Quilts, Quilts, and More Quilts!, Diana McClun & Laura Nownes

Rotary Cutting with Alex Anderson: Tips, Techniques, and Projects, Alex Anderson

Rx for Quilters, Susan Delaney-Mech

Say It with Quilts, Diana McClun & Laura Nownes

Scrap Quilts: The Art of Making Do, Roberta Horton

Setting Solutions, Sharyn Craig

Shadow Quilts, Patricia Magaret & Donna Slusser

Shadow Redwork™ with Alex Anderson: 24 Designs to Mix and Match, Alex Anderson

Show Me How to Machine Quilt: A Fun, No-Mark Approach, Kathy Sandbach

Simply Stars: Quilts That Sparkle, Alex Anderson

Skydyes: A Visual Guide to Fabric Painting, Mickey Lawler

Small Scale Quiltmaking: Precision, Proportion, and Detail, Sally Collins

Smashing Sets: Exciting Ways to Arrange Quilt Blocks, Margaret J. Miller

Snowflakes & Quilts, Paula Nadelstern

Soft-Edge Piecing: Add the Elegance of Appliqué to Traditional-Style Patchwork Design, Jinny Beyer

Special Delivery Quilts, Patrick Lose

Start Quilting with Alex Anderson, 2nd Edition: Six Projects for First-Time Quilters, Alex Anderson

Stitch 'n Flip Quilts: 14 Fantastic Projects, Valori Wells

Stripes In Quilts, Mary Mashuta

Strips 'n Curves: A New Spin on Strip Piecing, Louisa L. Smith

Thimbleberries Housewarming, A: 22 Projects for Quilters, Lynette Jensen

Through the Garden Gate: Quilters and Their Gardens, Jean Wells & Valori Wells

Tradition with a Twist: Variations on Your Favorite Quilts, Blanche Young & Dalene Young-Stone

Trapunto by Machine, Hari Walner

Travels with Peaky and Spike: Doreen Speckmann's Quilting Adventures, Doreen Speckmann

Visual Dance, The: Creating Spectacular Quilts, Joen Wolfrom

Wild Birds: Designs for Appliqué & Quilting, Carol Armstrong

Wildflowers: Designs for Appliqué and Quilting, Carol Armstrong

Women of Taste: A Collaboration Celebrating Quilt Artists and Chefs, Girls Incorporated

Yvonne Porcella: Art & Inspirations (sc): Art & Inspirations, Yvonne Porcella

For more information write for a free catalog:
C&T Publishing, Inc.
P.O. Box 1456
Lafayette, CA 94549
(800) 284-1114
e-mail: ctinfo@ctpub.com
website: www.ctpub.com

For quilting supplies:
Cotton Patch Mail Order
3405 Hall Lane, Dept.CTB
Lafayette, CA 94549
(800) 835-4418
(925) 283-7883
e-mail:quiltusa@yahoo.com
website: www.quiltusa.com

Note: Fabrics used in the quilts shown may not be currently available since fabric manufacturers keep most fabrics in print for only a short time.